THE
PREACHER'S PAPERBACK
LIBRARY

The Preacher's Paperback Library
Edmund A. Steimle, Consulting Editor

A Brief History
of Preaching

YNGVE BRILIOTH

1368

Translated by

Karl E. Mattson

FORTRESS PRESS • PHILADELPHIA

Translated from *Predikans historia*
by Yngve Brilioth
C. W. K. Gleerup, Lund, 1945

© 1965 by FORTRESS PRESS

Library of Congress Catalog Card Number 65-13256

8354B65   Printed in U.S.A.   UB996P

ABOUT THE
PREACHER'S PAPERBACK LIBRARY

The renewal of the church in our time has touched many aspects of parish life: liturgy and sacraments, biblical and theological concern, the place of the laity, work with small groups. But little has been said or done with regard to the renewal of the church in the pulpit.

The Preacher's Paperback Library is offered in the hope that it will contribute to the renewal of the preaching ministry. It will not stoop to providing "sermon starters" or other homiletical gimmicks. It will, rather, attempt to hold in balance the emphasis which contemporary theologians and biblical scholars lay upon the centrality of proclamation and the very practical concerns of theological students and parish pastors who are engaged in the demanding task of preparing sermons of biblical and theological depth which also speak to the contemporary world.

To that end, the series will provide reprints of fundamental homiletical studies not presently available and contemporary studies in areas of immediate concern to the preacher. Moreover, because the study of sermons themselves can be of invaluable help in every aspect of the preparation of the sermon, volumes of sermons with introductory notes will appear from time to time. The sermons will include reprints of outstanding preachers in the past as well as sermons by contemporary preachers who have given evidence both of depth and of imaginative gifts in communication. It is our hope that each volume in The Preacher's Paperback Library, prepared with the specific task of sermon preparation in mind, will contribute to the renewal of the preaching ministry.

We understand the present only in the light of developments in the past. This is as true of preaching as it is of every other area of knowledge or experience. One of the lacunae in contemporary homiletical literature is a brief but scholarly survey of the history of preaching. This translation, by the late Dr. Karl E. Mattson, of *A Brief History of Preaching* by Yngve Brilioth (1891-1959), originally published in Sweden as *Predikans historia,* is a valuable contribution to the field. It is eminently readable and perceptive. The contemporary preacher will better understand his task for the reading and study of this book.

The scope of the subject is so vast that the author has, understandably, set limits for his study. The emphasis is on the development of preaching on the continent; little is said of the development of preaching in the new world. The need remains for a brief survey of the history of preaching in America; meanwhile, we welcome this thoughtful volume as a prerequisite to any study of the history of preaching. Archbishop Brilioth, who is known to us all for his monumental *Eucharistic Faith and Practice,* has in this volume placed all preachers and students of preaching in the debt of his massively brilliant historical and theological insight.

The appendix to this volume, prepared from two chapters in Archbishop Brilioth's original work, presents a rapid review of the development of preaching in Sweden. It is a valuable piece of scholarship, containing material not otherwise available in English. It was prepared by Dr. Mattson immediately before his untimely death in late 1964.

In the preparation of this volume for publication in the United States, we are indebted not only to the translator, but also to two of my students for their valuable assistance. The Rev.

Morris J. Niedenthal has provided an annotated bibliography on the history of preaching, and the Rev. Dr. Clair E. Johnson has prepared the index. Footnote references have been prepared with the intent of aiding the English reader.

EDMUND A. STEIMLE

Union Theological Seminary
New York, New York
Epiphany, 1965

CONTENTS

ONE

From Synagogue to Church:
The Three Basic Elements

The Cultic Address in the Old Testament

The well-known account of how Jesus taught in the synagogue at Nazareth is found in Luke 4:16b-21:

> And he went to the synagogue, as his custom was, on the sabbath day. And he stood up to read; and there was given to him the book of the prophet Isaiah. He opened the book and found the place where it was written, "The Spirit of the Lord is upon me, because he has anointed me to preach good news to the poor. He has sent me to proclaim release to the captives and recovery of sight to the blind, to set at liberty those who are oppressed, to proclaim the acceptable year of the Lord." And he closed the book and gave it back to the attendant, and sat down; and the eyes of all in the synagogue were fixed on him. And he began to say to them, "Today this scripture has been fulfilled in your hearing."

The account continues by relating the reaction of the hearers. They wondered at the gracious words which proceeded out of his mouth and they said, "Is not this Joseph's son?" Jesus' vehement reply, which culminated in the words, "No prophet is acceptable in his own country," led the people to drive him out of their city and to threaten his life.

This narrative is a useful starting point in a study of the history of preaching. Insufficient attention has been given to its significance. Here is the bridge between the Christian sermon

1

and the proclamation in the synagogue. The use of the oral lecture in the service is a trait that unites Judaism and Christianity. Where, in the world of religion, can we find a counterpart? Careful research could probably find isolated parallels. The oral exposition of the Koran is given a similar status in Islam, a mark of affinity probably traceable to Islam's dependence on biblical religion. Instruction has certainly appeared in all of the higher religions, as, surely, has some form of missionary preaching. Interpretations of cultic legends and words of exhortation seem to have appeared occasionally in the mystery religions, but we have only very fragmentary information concerning such exposition. Rite, sacrifice, and liturgical formula have generally been dominant in the cult. Only Judaism and Christendom make the freely spoken word, the personal testimony, an essential portion of the holy acts of the cult. It therefore becomes necessary to examine more closely into the connection between the synagogue and the church. To what degree is the Christian sermon a direct continuation of the exposition of Scripture in the synagogue? Is it possible to establish a causal relationship that leads from the Jewish cultic address to the pattern taken by Christian preaching?

If by preaching we mean the exposition of a holy writing as an act of the cult, we can hardly identify the Jewish sermon until post-exilic times. It is in the synagogue service that the Jewish sermon assumes its form. The synagogue, having arisen as a substitute for the temple, originated cultic forms of a wholly different character. Nevertheless, preaching, in a broader sense, had appeared much earlier in Israel. The historical books of the Old Testament contain many examples of spiritual discourses delivered by leaders of the people—judges, priests, and prophets. In every instance, these discourses had their background in a concrete historical situation, as in the farewell address Joshua delivered in the presence of the assembled congregation (Joshua, chapter 24). At times the discourses were united with the acts of the cult and thus assumed a more direct sacral character. While we may presuppose the existence of a specific rhetorical or literary tradition in this context, we are not dealing here with the interpretation of Scripture in its proper sense. Not infrequently, however, as in Joshua's farewell address, the starting point appears to have been a recital of God's dealings with his people in times past, as well as a recollection of the covenant which made Israel the chosen people. These reminders then became the basis for an exhortation which emphasized the duties of the people. The same pattern appears in the address of Mattatias to his sons in I Macc. 2:49-68 and some of the addresses in Acts.

Prophecy has been even more significant for the tradition of the holy address and the development of veneration for the holy word. Like cultic speech, it emerged out of a sacral form, out of speaking in oracles.[1] It placed ecstatic inspiration in the service of both religious renewal and the personal life of the spirit. In its most proper sense, prophecy asserted itself as a holy address, a compelling word of God put into the mouth of his servants and messengers. In recent biblical research it has been customary to emphasize the ecstatic and revelatory elements in the testimony of the prophets. Another era will, perhaps, pay more attention to the rational proclamation, which assuredly is no small part of the writings of the major prophets, and search for traces of a homiletical tradition in this context also. For our purposes it is especially important to emphasize the process by which the church took a legacy from the prophets and carried forward in its preaching the same high claims as those which appeared in the proclamation of the prophets. Unquestionably, a clear line extends from Old Testament prophecy to the sermon in the church. To trace the contours of this line, especially in the New Testament era and the post-apostolic one,

[1] For a discussion of the prophets as preachers, see Johannes Lindblom, *Prophecy in Ancient Israel* (Philadelphia: Fortress Press, 1962), p 311.

would be a fascinating task for further research. The line appears most clearly, perhaps, in Jesus' sermon at Nazareth: here the synagogal sermon is the immediate background. It is evident that the sermon in the church also has a heritage, if a less direct one, from the prophet's majestic judgments and oracles. The Christian preacher's claim that he is a bearer of the word of God and not only an expositor, and the veneration for the spoken word which is an essential characteristic of the Christian life of worship, would hardly be imaginable without the pattern of prophecy.

Bible reading as such has certainly had more signficance for preaching than any continuity between text and sermon which could be uncovered by exegesis or patristic studies. Every preacher who has entered deeply into the writings of the Old Testament prophets must have been led to a higher conception of his task as well as to a deeper sense of responsibility in the face of his call to be a servant of the word. The story of the call of Jeremiah has certainly been as significant for the history of preaching as the story of the call of Isaiah has been for the history of the cult. Surely we should be able to discover a connection between the use of the Old Testament and respect for the service of the word. As an ideal and a source of inspiration, Old Testament prophecy has always been an influence of the utmost importance in the development of Christian preaching. This appears most clearly, as we subsequently shall show, in Reformed preaching.

The Sermon in the Synagogue

The relation of Christian preaching to the service in the synagogue is more obvious but less profound than its relation to Old Testament prophecy. The reading of Scripture and the exposition of it were parts of the service, together with liturgical sentences, prayers, and benedictions—for example, *Shema, Shemoneh Esreh,* and *Kedushah*[2]—and psalms and hymns. The law and the prophets were both read on the sabbath day. When Hebrew ceased to be the spoken language, an interpretation became necessary as a supplement to the reading. Although this interpretation could be expanded into a detailed exposition, it usually assumed the character of a rather informal lecture. Thus originated the sermon in the synagogue.[3]

This sermon also, has had its own history. It began as an instructive exposition. When Ezra read the law (Nehemiah, chapter 8), he was assisted by the Levites who taught the people. For a long time there was no distinction between preaching and teaching; teaching was the usual term in the synagogue, used also to describe Jesus' proclamation. He "taught" in the synagogue (Mark 1:21), he sat down on the mountain and "taught them, saying" (Matt. 5:1-2). Out of this teaching in the synagogue there arose by degrees the rich expository literature which we know as the Targum, the Midrash, and the Haggadah. The substance of the tradition grew and scriptural exposition was changed into a study of Scripture which often forgot the spirit for the letter.

[2] [*Shema* ("Hear")—the first word of the basic Jewish affirmation of faith, made up of Deut. 6:4-8, 11:13-22 and Num. 15:37-42, beginning, "Hear, O Israel."

Shemoneh Esreh ("Eighteen")—the eighteen (now nineteen) benedictions spoken at each of the three daily services in the synagogue; sometimes called *Amidah* ("standing") because the congregation stands during its recital.

Kedushah ("Sanctification")—a response to the third benediction of the *Shemoneh Esreh,* made up principally of Isa. 6:3, Ezek. 3:12, and Ps. 146:10. The *Trisagion* of the Christian liturgy is probably derived from the *Kedushah.*—TRANSLATOR.]

[3] [George Foot Moore, *Judaism* (Cambridge: Harvard Univ. Press, 1932), I, 305-307 speaks of homilies in the synagogue service. W. O. E. Oesterley, *The Jewish Background of the Christian Liturgy* (Oxford: Clarendon Press, 1925) speaks of the exposition as one of the elements in pre-Christian Jewish worship on pp. 41-42; he treats of its influence on early forms of Christian worship on pp. 111-121.—TRANSLATOR.]

Soon a longer, more freely structured exposition was added to the reading of the *haftarah* from the prophetic writings and the later historical books. The law was divided into *parashiyoth*.[4] This kind of exposition was by no means obligatory; it could be omitted if a suitable expositor were not available. Reader and expositor could be the same person, as in the synagogue at Nazareth, or two different persons. In many places by the time of Jesus, the exposition which was connected to the reading of the prophets had taken on the character of an informal lecture, a sermon with an edifying purpose usually ending with a "word of comfort." The speaker no longer interpreted the whole of the *haftarah* read, but was content to use it as a starting point.

Scriptural exposition was not a privilege assigned to any specific office. It could be delegated to anyone who had the capacity for it. In the synagogues of the diaspora, a traveling stranger could often be asked to perform this service as a welcome change in the spiritual diet. As a result, it could be said of Paul following his conversion that "in the synagogues immediately he proclaimed Jesus, saying, 'He is the Son of God'" (Acts 9:20). Paul and Barnabas in Antioch of Pisidia, when they had come to the synagogue on the sabbath day, could be invited by the leader of the synagogue to speak "the word of exhortation" to the people (Acts 13:15). Thus the oldest Christian preaching, in the congregations of the Jewish dispersion, related itself to the tradition of synagogal worship.

The account of Jesus' visit to the synagogue at Nazareth is, doubtless, one of the most vivid pictures we have of the Jewish service of the time. Its details are supported by other knowledge we possess concerning the cultic forms used in the synagogue. Very probably no specific series of *haftarah* had yet been estab-

---

[4] [In Babylonia, the Torah was divided into fifty-four sections, each called a *parashah*; when one section was read each week, the Torah was

lished for the readings on the sabbath day, but a certain limitation was present, since only the book of Isaiah was given to the reader. It is stated that as Jesus opened the book he found the place, Isaiah 61. From this we cannot establish whether or not the passage was in any way previously appointed for reading or if Jesus chose it by chance or deliberately. In careful conformity to custom, Jesus sat down as the interpretation began. In this manner the custom continued for hundreds of years. We may ask ourselves, was it in keeping with this custom that the bishops of the ancient church seated themselves to deliver their homilies from the throne behind the holy table?

The exposition as Luke renders it is short, "Today this scripture has been fulfilled in your hearing"; but from what follows we can by no means conclude that this was the whole address. That they "wondered at the gracious words which proceeded out of his mouth" seems to imply a longer presentation out of which this sentence alone etched itself in the memory of the hearers.

It has been customary for the history of preaching to go back no further than the words spoken by Jesus himself. This may be legitimate insofar as the Christian proclamation is essentially the message concerning Jesus Christ and God's act in him, the message of the fulfillment of the gospel. By this emphasis, however, we have doubtless shortened the perspective and cut the lines of communication between the Old Testament and the church. The Gospels, which furnish the classic texts for preaching, are essentially *kerygmata,* the first fruits of the Christian proclamation. The relation between Jesus' preaching and preaching in the church contains problems which will perhaps never be clearly focussed. But we can ask the question, to what degree has the tradition of the synagogue left its imprint on other words of Jesus as well as on other stories in the Gospels? Jesus' use of the word of Scripture from the Old

read through once a year. In Palestine, the Torah was read through once every three years; the Babylonian custom prevailed in later times, however.—TRANSLATOR.]

Testament is related to this question.[5] The problems contained in Jesus' use of the parable also belong in this context. We have already pointed out that both the exposition of Scripture in the synagogue and the Old Testament religious address have influenced the addresses found in Acts. The religious addresses in Acts surely are not sermons proper, but their structure is nevertheless reminiscent of the synagogue proclamation. An investigation of these problems would naturally find its source material in the letters of the apostles, and perhaps also in the Apocalypse. Beyond this, the Apocalypse points to another pattern of relationship in the history of preaching. Here we face the question: to what degree did the oral proclamation in the ancient church contain an apocalyptic element related to the Jewish prototype?

Primary Elements: Liturgical, Exegetical, Prophetic

Our immediate task is to seek to establish Jesus' sermon in the synagogue at Nazareth as the most important link in the golden chain which unites the Jewish proclamation and the Christian sermon and which creates a deep continuity in the history of the biblical revelation by this use of both the old and the new word. Three basic elements seem to emerge with distinct clarity: I wish to identify them as the liturgical, the exegetical, and the prophetic. The order in which they are here presented is not intended as an evaluation.

The *liturgical* element: Jesus' sermon was delivered within the context of the Jewish service. The sermon was an accepted, traditional, and prescribed part of this service, even though it was not obligatory. At times, the sermon in the synagogue certainly did emancipate itself from the cultic context, but when

[5] J. Leipoldt, *Der Gottesdienst der ältesten Kirche* (1937), p. 15, thinks some of Jesus' addresses especially those related to passages from the Old Testament, are fragments of synagogal sermons.

we meet it in the Gospels and in the Acts of the Apostles it is within this compass. Here we are confronted by one of the most distinctive characteristics of both the synagogal and the Christian sermon.

The *exegetical* element: Jesus spoke from a text, the question of whether it depended on his own choice or not being of no consequence. Gradually the freedom of choice in the synagogue was limited more and more by a developing order of prescribed pericopes. We can observe a similar development within the church. This development, however, is less significant than the essential principle that the edifying discourse have its roots in the exposition of a text, and that the sermon, after ceasing to be a direct commentary on a text, continue to have as its starting point a word of Scripture. One of the most essential guarantees of the sermon's religious content is found in this rootage. Within both Judaism and Christianity, the exposition of a text always faces the possibility of going astray. It can become cluttered with a growing body of traditional material which obscures rather than clarifies the meaning of the words, and which acts as an obstacle in the establishment of a personal relationship between the interpreter and his text. Exposition has a dangerous tendency to stop at the letter and to find hidden meanings under the surface of the text—indeed, allegorizing is one of the hereditary taints of scriptural preaching, and here the Jewish legacy has not been neutralized by the literary tradition of Christian antiquity. On the other hand, the exposition of Scripture's historical context makes valuable contributions. When seen at its best, the Old Testament proclamation, as well as the sermon in the synagogue, rose to a presentation of the tremendous continuity of the history of revelation. In this context, Stephen's address in the seventh chapter of Acts gives occasion for further reflection. Nor did the proclamation in the synagogue lack the perspective of pastoral care, since it related Scripture to the hearer and out of Scripture brought forth the

9

motifs and the words of consolation which were applicable to his situation.

The *prophetic* element: "Today this scripture has been fulfilled in your hearing." The content of Jesus' preaching was summed up in this prophetic declaration, which retained the characteristic crisp, lapidary style of the oracles. The sermon was prophetic in the deepest sense, inasmuch as it is the essential nature of prophecy to speak to the present with divine authority and to transform the historical revelation into a contemporaneous, dynamic reality. The captivating feature of this summary account of Jesus' sermon is that it shows us how the prophetic word, with its creative, elemental religious power and with its supernatural demands, finds a place within the framework of the sabbath sermon in the synagogue while at the same time victoriously breaking these shackles. Jesus' words have thus given the highest authorization to the claim of the Christian preacher that he also stands in the prophetic succession. Furthermore, they have placed upon the preacher the overwhelming responsibility of being more than a commentator on a text. He is to interpret every text so that out of its swaddling clothes the Lord of Scripture and the fulfiller of prophecy appears as the contemporary teacher and Lord. This Lord is the one who gives to every text its interpretation and its address for every time and place; he is the one who gives to every text its eternal content.

Secondary Elements

Patient research should, through an analytical investigation, be able to discover the basic outline of the norms which may be used in evaluating the various epochs and forms of Christian preaching as it developed through the centuries. Our imagination is immediately struck by the boundless quantity of material and by the hopelessly extensive work required. What has been preserved and printed from ancient and medieval times comprises a whole library by itself. The homiletical literature since the time of the Reformation is prodigious in dimension. To the printed sources we must also add handwritten material in an inestimable quantity. Nor is the area of investigation limited to the extant sources. The conscientious scholar is met at every step of the way by critical and literary-historical problems. And, if he has understood his task correctly, he must conceive his eventual goal as the task of investigating and grasping a reality which lies beyond the available manuscripts, a reality which cannot be contained in the prison net of literary-historical method. He must seek to grasp the act of proclamation as a living reality in which the personality of the preacher, the situation of the hearer, the character of the time, the framework of the service, and the very room where the word is spoken are included as essential factors. The manuscripts at hand, if not scrutinized in terms of intention, can give only a weak and pale picture of this living reality.

The presentation which we have begun here seeks to move in another direction which, perhaps, cannot make the claim of being scientific in the sense in which pedantic wisdom has defined the method of science. This study seeks to present and to defend a thesis which may appear to be rash, namely, that Jesus' sermon in the synagogue at Nazareth gives us the key to the history of Christian preaching through the ages. This implies that the sermon in the Christian church, as a unique oratorical act and a form of speech which by degrees has attained a clearly defined form, is most profoundly influenced by these three component elements or principles: the liturgical, the exegetical, and the prophetic. A study of the history of the sermon must, first of all, keep in mind the development and interrelatedness of these principles.

It is evident that the establishment of this thesis must be followed by certain reservations. The most immediate, perhaps, is the reservation that it is only in the cult sermon proper that the three principles can be united. In every age the church has, nevertheless, practiced missionary preaching and in most denominations the sermon has also been given a place in purely non-liturgical services. It is not within the province of this study to renew the scholastically oriented discussion concerning the essence of the sermon. A definition which covers all of the manifold types of preaching or all forms of spiritual address which have appeared in Christendom must of necessity be so inane as to lack real worth. What is to be included in the concept of the sermon must always continue to be a question of taste. It is, however, necessary for us to give our attention to the sermon in its specific uniqueness, as a form of address which has not only developed within the worship life of the church, but developed such a fixed form in this context that it can be differentiated from other rhetorical types. This unique rhetorical character, recognizable in this usual pattern, has been created within the context of the service by the special needs of the worshiping congregation and by the liturgical environment in which it has been placed. The word sermon can be given various shades of emphasis. It can be a term of contempt or of appreciation, but it also denotes something distinct and it is this uniqueness which we must grasp. After this form has been once developed it can be maintained without this specific liturgical orientation; nevertheless, according to this observation, when the liturgical context is absent the character of the sermon is easily modified and the line of demarcation between preaching and spiritual discourse very quickly becomes fluid. We must, therefore, acknowledge the decisive significance of the liturgical principle in the development of preaching.

It can also be established that catechetical preaching hardly belongs in a sermon which is wholly determined by the three component elements we have mentioned. A study of the history of preaching proves that at specified times, preaching has had a catechetical orientation; its purpose has been to foster and to teach the congregation. We have already noted that this is true of synagogal preaching. It is also likely that the same circumstances prevailed in apostolic times and this can be substantiated by such passages as "Obey your leaders and submit to them; for they are keeping watch over your souls" (Heb. 13:17). ["Leaders" reads "teachers" in the Swedish New Testament.] But to the extent that the church has arrived at a prescribed order of service, it has also differentiated between proper catechetical work and preaching. This by no means precludes the fact that an instructional element has always been present and must always maintain its place, but in the fully developed sermon it can be included within the compass of the prophetic element and insofar as the basic concern is instruction in Scripture it can also be included in the exegetical element. Overemphasis on the instructional aspects of the sermon, however, distorts the essential character of preaching in the service. Such an overemphasis has appeared from time to time, prompted by specific circumstances. If our investigation is not to distort the reality, we must class the catechetical element as the most important of the subsidiary elements to which we shall give our attention.

Certain other secondary motifs may be included under some aspect of the three basic elements. This is true both of the paranetic motif, which we will discover especially in the preaching of the ancient church, and of the interest in the care of souls, which must always maintain its place and which emerges with especial power in times of spiritual renewal and deepening. Both paranesis, the proclamation of ethical admonition, and the interest in the care of souls are legitimate forms of the prophetic sermon, inasmuch as this sermon's primary concern is to orient the Christian message to the present and to supply the message with current and personal content.

A secondary factor which sometimes emerges strongly may be called the scholastic homiletical tradition. This tradition, which one age inherited from another, was a specific preaching technique, which often competed very noticeably with the more basic elements in establishing the pattern of preaching.

Strong arguments could surely be presented against this unmethodical method of beginning an investigation, even which can be characterized as a sketchy survey, with ready-made categories of this type. One could say that the completed interpretation is apparently inherent in the method, or that the method itself implies an evaluation or preconceived idea of what the sermon is and should be. Such a presentation must vary according to the observer's presuppositions, his churchly tradition; a similar investigation attempted in a Reformed milieu would have started with different premises. Nevertheless, these objections may be answered by saying that every historical presentation, no matter how carefully it seeks to be objective, is determined by the scholar's personal presuppositions. The exposition which we present here seeks primarily to grasp the uniqueness of the sermon; the study of the sermon's historical genesis becomes the most significant resource. The three basic elements are given the character of a working hypothesis which proves its worth to the degree that it is found useful. Without the guidance of such a hypothesis, it would be impossible for us to find our course through homiletical history's confusing and insufficiently charted seas. Here our task is not to give a carefully balanced orientation to the whole tremendous area. We must, first of all, approach the sermon itself, as it has developed within the church, a rhetorical form which is unique to Christian worship. In this task, it is especially necessary to fix our attention on the development and retention of this distinctiveness. The most highly literate and cultured preachers have not always been the best examples of this distinctiveness. The rhetorical traditions of non-Christian and nonchurchly culture have been very much alive in the history of preaching and sometimes they have also wished to place the art of spiritual discourse under

14

their dominion. But such influences—we shall call them literary sub-motifs—have always been dangerous and have always made it more difficult for the sermon to become clearly conscious of its own essence.

When we derived the three basic elements from the account of Jesus' sermon in the synagogue at Nazareth, we by no means intended to give them a normative character. To be sure, they have a profound symbolic content as the classic example of the connection between the service in the synagogue and the service in the church. If it becomes evident that these three elements present a fruitful method for our investigation, their derivation from the Lucan pericope will certainly be worthy of consideration as expressing the fact that the elements which have determined and created the Christian sermon have deep roots in the history of the revelation which meets us in the Bible.

TWO

The Greek Homily

The Beginnings

The simulated address played a significant role in the historical writings of antiquity. It was a usual medium of expression for authors, and only in exceptional circumstances can we consider the extant chronicles as factual reports of what was actually said. It is generally supposed that we should evaluate the occasional addresses in Acts in this context and that they cannot therefore be considered as examples of the oldest Christian preaching. It is, nevertheless, not outside the realm of possibility that to a certain degree they do reflect well-remembered reports by those who heard. They do not, however, appear as cultic addresses to brethren in the faith, but are rather directed to the Jews and the heathen. In every instance, it is important that we know Luke's or the unknown editor's understanding of how the apostles should have spoken. We have already noted that some of the addresses show a direct dependence on the preaching of the Old Testament; the writings which the early preachers knew and used were the law and the prophets. These writings found their fulfillment in the message of the resurrected Savior, a message which, at this time, was yet a living word rather than a written document. Furthermore an obvious linkage with the prototypes of antiquity appears at this point alongside the Old Testament tradition. We notice rationally oriented, apologetic thought patterns in the addresses which are directed to the heathen, and these patterns are continued in the Epistle to Diognetus, in Justin and Athenagoras.

Special attention has been given to Paul's address at the

Areopagus (Acts, chapter 17) because of Eduard Norden's famous study *Agnostos Theos* (1913) which seeks to show that we have here an evident relationship to the religious address of antiquity. This address, according to Norden, is related to certain types which were created during the syncretistic era of the Caesars. The forms have been mediated by Hellenistic Judaism and Stoicism. The Stoic diatribe was given a continued existence in early Christian preaching as soon as the sermon assumed a literary form on Hellenistic soil, the first time that Christian preaching became dependent on a nonbiblical literary tradition. This is the first time we may speak of a literary submotif.

The addresses in the Acts of the Apostles are not usually presented as sermons to a congregation. To what degree did the teaching of the apostles assume the character of a sermon in the oldest Christian congregations? The short reports and interpretations in Acts and in the Epistles, which most obviously suggest themselves, may well satisfy the imagination but their content is hardly material for scholarly investigation. It is evident that "prophecy" often assumed the character of a very rational exposition, related to the Old Testament writings, and because of this it exhibited a certain exegetical orientation. This orientation, however, found a strong rival in ecstatic speaking. It is obvious that the address, whether as prophecy or as textual exposition, even though it was without rules and by no means connected with a permanent office, had a place within the context of the cult. At least it is possible to suppose that certain formally conceived passages like the doxologies in the Epistles (e.g., Rom. 16:25 ff., I Tim. 1:17), preserve the memory of preaching, where as yet no definite line of demarcation had separated it from corporate prayer and liturgy. Many sections of the Epistles, especially of the Pastorals, must have had counterparts in the oral proclamation. Here we also discover some of the oldest evidences of expository and catechetical preaching (I Tim. 4:13).

In the earliest Christian literature, the written sermon and the literary epistle have been united. The time for creating specific forms is yet distant. Charismatic prophecy and edifying teaching are given a more important place than pure textual interpretation, especially on Greek soil. In the apostolic and post-apostolic eras it is very probable that we must reckon with an antithesis between a Gentile Christianity on the one hand, in which the type of worship had to a degree been influenced by the religious syncretism of the Roman Empire, in which charismatic speech was dominant, and in which there were no fixed forms and on the other hand a Jewish Christianity, which was dependent on the tradition of the synagogue and in which from the very beginning the proclamation was usually based on the interpretation of a text.[1] As yet the text was primarily a living witness, the kerygma of what the preacher himself had experienced. The evangelical prophecy was basically an oral message concerning the fulfillment of Old Testament prophecy in the gospel of grace and truth which came through Jesus Christ. This is its greatest contribution to the tradition of Christian preaching.

The sources for a history of preaching in the post-apostolic era are very scanty. It is possible that a thorough consideration of the literary documents from the second century would be able to put together faint descriptions and similarities and thus make some contribution toward a clearer picture. During this time the Greek homily and its counterparts within the Semitic churches came into being. We meet the word *homilia* itself for the first time in Ignatius' letter to Polycarp as a description of the word spoken in the congregation; most exactly, it refers to an address of admonition. In Hellenistic usage, the term had

---

[1] J. Leipoldt, *Der Gottesdienst der ältesten Kirche* (1937), pp. 30 ff. Leipoldt finds tendencies in the Greek service in Corinth, as it is described in I Corinthians. which show dependence upon the mystery cults as well as conscientious opposition to them.

already acquired the meaning "instructive address," but it is hardly advisable to deduce any far-reaching conclusions concerning the nature of the early sermon. The task of preaching was an important factor in the development of the office of the ministry, and this fact has not always been sufficiently appreciated. In *The Teaching of the Twelve Apostles* (Didache), we meet traveling apostles, prophets, and teachers at a time when it was already necessary to distinguish between true and false prophets. But when it says that the Christian should day and night remember him who speaks God's word to him, it is not referring to the prophet. In *The Shepherd of Hermas* there is a description of a man who had the gift of the spirit who came to a congregation and was allowed to speak. Parallel with the development of church order and the cult, there was also a similar development in preaching; the cessation of the charismatic gifts compelled greater attention to the outward forms. In the later ancient church the task of preaching was the bishop's prerogative, as the possessor of the office of teaching; this task was not necessarily united with the office of presbyter, even though the presbyter could also be given the responsibility of preaching.[2]

In the document which is usually described as the first sermon available to us, the so-called Second Letter of Clement, there is hardly any trace of the extraordinary gifts of the Spirit. It is a sober little tract concerning Christ's deed of love which ought to compel the Christian to confess him not only in word but also in deed, in the fear of God, without fear of martyrdom, and in expectation of the reward which awaits the faithful. It asserts that baptism requires the Christian to be penitent, and it speaks of the resurrection of the body and the coming glory. The letter is thought to be addressed to Rome or Corinth since it accompanies the First Letter of Clement as an appendix and

[2] Cf. H. B. Swete (ed.), *Essays on the Early History of the Church and the Ministry* (New York: Macmillan Co., 1921), pp. 229, 236.

is dated between A.D. 100 and A.D. 150. Its form is surely that of a sermon: it begins with an address to the brethren, exhorting them not only to pay attention to the prophet at the service, "but when we have gone home, we should bear in mind the Lord's commands," and it ends with a formally constructed and enraptured doxology "To the only invisible God,"

> the Father of truth, who dispatched to us the Saviour and prince of immortality, through whom he also disclosed to us the truth and the heavenly life—to him be glory forever and ever. Amen.[3]

The liturgical quotation does not continue further. The letter certainly was delivered at a service in the congregation and to that extent it stands as a sermon. The length of the document suggests that the sermon was edited after it had been preached, perhaps in order to make it more appropriate as a written letter. An exegetical orientation is not lacking. But it is characterized by a certain primitive obscureness. The document starts with a prophetic word and contains several citations from the Old Testament. The sermon on which it was based was preceded by a lection from the Bible, but no specific pericope is exegeted. Besides quotations from Matthew and Luke, noncanonical words of Jesus are cited: the living message has not yet been completely confined in the written Gospels. We also note a definite need for a deeper anchorage in the written word of God as a counterbalance to other influences.

Prophecy has been silenced and replaced by teaching and a sober paranesis which makes a very poor impression on contemporary readers, even though it does give an impression of the early Christian mood of alienation from the world and of expectation of the heavenly crown of victory. Some have taken

---

[3] Cyril C. Richardson (ed.), "An Anonymous Sermon, Commonly Called Clement's Second Letter to the Corinthians," trans. Cyril C. Richardson, *Early Christian Fathers* ("Library of Christian Classics," Vol. I [Philadelphia: Westminster Press, 1953]), pp. 200, 202.

it for granted that the Second Letter of Clement had as its literary prototype the popular philosophical essay, especially the Stoic diatribe, but this is highly doubtful.

The artificiality of a sermon by Melito of Sardis stands in sharp contrast to this appealing and simple presentation. Melito's sermon is the second available source concerning the nature of Christian preaching in the second century. Discovered in a papyrus, it has only recently become available.[4] The sermon was delivered on the first day of Easter, and deals with Jesus' sacrificial death. Melito was a quartodeciman and therefore celebrated Easter on the fourteenth of Nisan. The massing of forced antitheses and typological applications of Old Testament subjects makes the sermon difficult and unpalatable. Melito apparently sought to assume the role of prophet in a period when prophecy had ceased—at least to the degree that it had not become the prerogative of the Montanists. Tertullian's critique of Melito's rhetorical excesses is not without merit. Melito's rhetoric does, however, differentiate itself from Greek oratory. Various expressions are reminiscent of earlier liturgical texts and we are tempted by the hypothesis that we have here an imitation of a special prophetic stance which had developed even as prophecy itself had ceased to be spontaneous. Melito draws an interesting connection with a reading from Exodus before his sermon: "The text from the Hebrew Exodus has been read and the word of mystery has been explained; how the sheep has been offered, and how the people have been delivered!" We are left in doubt as to the meaning of "explained"—perhaps an explanation was given by the expositor or preacher before the sermon itself? The Old Testament is still cited as the original holy document and various expressions from the New Testament are recalled but not quoted.

[4] Campbell Bonner (ed.), *The Homily on the Passion by Bishop Melito of Sardis* ("Studies and Documents," Vol. XII, 1940). This discussion is dependent upon a review by A. C. Headlam in *The Guardian,* December 27, 1940.

The liturgical context of preaching, which appears more clearly in Melito than in the Second Letter of Clement, is directly confirmed in Justin Martyr's classic description of the primary Christian service in chapter 67 of the First Apology. The gathering for worship was held on the day of the sun when everyone from city and country came together. The writings of the apostles and prophets were read. When the reading was concluded "the leader, through an address gave an exhortation to follow these beautiful examples." The corporate prayer and the celebration of the Lord's Supper followed immediately thereafter. The word leader, of course, refers to the bishop; the congregation is no longer concerned with the assistance of the prophet. The expressions which refer to the address most probably refer to a paranetic homily related to the text which had been read. Justin's testimony concerning the sermon as an integral part of the Sunday worship is very significant, since the reference is to the complete high mass, the main outlines of which have always been familiar to us.

From Origen to the Cappadocian Fathers

The Greek homily rises from its obscure beginnings in the second century in a series of bold impulses to its maximum height in the preachers of the fourth century. The first new impulse comes from the exegetical homilies of Origen (c. 185-c. 254). It was through him that exegesis and preaching were so firmly united that throughout the history of the ancient church and long afterwards they remained intertwined. In his vast literary legacy, which has been preserved until our own time and which is only a part of his original production, the homily occupies a prominent position, a position which, nevertheless, is secondary to his almost superhuman exegetical production.

The one hundred seventy-five homilies extant are based for

the most part on Old Testament texts, excepting the thirty-nine homilies from Luke. They have the character of a running exposition of the text, whether because they have been delivered consecutively on the biblical books, which surely is probable and which was possible in an era when a prescribed order of pericopes was not known, or because they are individual sermons delivered in various contexts which have been combined into a series.

When Origen was ordained as a presbyter in Caesarea, approximately A.D. 230 (also the year of his lifelong exile), he had long been a preacher. For him, ordination was merely an enlargement of the teaching office which he had earlier (A.D. 214) been prevailed upon to accept by the invitation of the bishop of Jerusalem and Caesarea. That locale had observed the primitive practice which allowed anyone—ordained or not—who was gifted with the spirit to address the congregation, in accordance with the practice in the synagogue. In Alexandria, however, such a practice was considered a great violation of churchly order.

Although Origen's homilies certainly took their place and their context from the service, their form was scarcely influenced by this orientation. The catechetical element appears much more significantly in the sermons that were delivered at the service of the catechumens, where the circle of hearers was larger than the circle of the faithful who participated in the holy mysteries. The mysteries could not be divulged to the uninitiated according to the principle established by the developing *Disciplina Arcani*. The presentation proceeds sedately, interpreting verse by verse, and ends rather arbitrarily in a final doxology, but neither the cultic context nor the confinement to a text enslaved the expositor. He found means of making the most trivial Old Testament text the bearer of a deep, esoteric wisdom. Eusebius quotes the sharp critique which Porphyry directed against Origen as a disciple of Ammonius Saccas, who—in spite of his Greek training—had degenerated to the level of barbaric religion. Eusebius further names the Stoics, Kairemon and Cornutus, among Origen's philosophic teachers: "From these he learned the allegorical method of interpretation taken from the Greek mysteries and (he) transferred the use of the method to the Jewish Scriptures." The discovery was not new; Paul could allegorize concerning Mount Sinai (Gal. 4:25) and Philo had used this art of interpretation with the skill of a master.

As it now reached its perfection in Origen, the basic motivations for allegory were, on the one hand, the Stoic tradition and, on the other hand, the constraint which the dominant position of the Old Testament laid upon the preacher. When the literal meaning of the unquestioned holy text gave little nourishment for the edifying meditation, the allegorical interpretation was allowed to take over—after both the literal and the moral content had been emptied of their real possibilities. As a result, the careful philological scrutiny of exegesis was abruptly transformed into an uninhibited spiritualization. "The dearly beloved child has many names," according to Origen; the hidden meaning must be discovered, one must reflect more carefully, one must think deeper and higher, one must see the divine, the inexpressible. When we consider the revealed word of God we must come to the conclusion that something lies hidden beneath the uninteresting laws, the naive stories, and the accounts of bloody battles. As far as external form was concerned, the Roman and Greek laws were vastly superior to the laws which God himself had given the chosen people: only the spiritual interpretation could make the superiority of the divine law evident. Thus the oxen in the text must be a sign of earthly desires, the sheep of foolish thoughts, and doves of dangerous fancies. Thus the account of how Rebecca came to the well included a profound lesson on how man must daily come to the well of the Scripture and draw out the overflow of the Spirit.

For Origen, allegory was doubtless the means by which he presented the message of the gospel as he understood it. It was his method of prophesying. But it is disheartening to note that the first great exegete in the history of preaching made the word of Scripture the bearer of a quite unbiblical message and introduced a method of interpretation into the tradition of the church which led exegetical preaching on the false path of allegory for hundreds of years.

The great transformation which the church experienced in the fourth century also changed the character of the sermon, which continued to be a liturgical act but was fitted into the developed order of the service even more solidly than had previously been the case. It followed the lections, which usually were three in number, and naturally enough it sought to establish a connection with the texts which had been read. The church year was yet in the process of formation but the great festivals and the more sharply differentiated seasons circumscribed the choice of subject, which otherwise could include anything in heaven or on earth. As a rule the extant liturgies do not mention the sermon, but we have other proofs of its place in the service.[5] Thus we are made aware through the Apostolic Constitutions that preaching most usually occurred at the celebration of the Sunday Eucharist and also on Ember days and martyrs' days. During Chrysostom's time in Antioch, in keeping with the old spirit of charismatic freedom, it still could happen that several short presentations followed each other, the bishop's last of all. Preaching thus blossomed into one of its most productive periods.

The great preachers of antiquity often preached daily, and in consequence they left a tremendous homiletical legacy. Even though various types developed during this period,

---

[5] In some relatively late sources on the history of the Byzantine liturgy, preaching is designated by the Greek word for teaching. In a liturgy from the Exarchate of Pontus, the Greek word for homily is used when the part of the service which follows the Gospel lection is mentioned. In a note from the seventh century, the following sentence appeared in Greek: "The leader teaches the word of godliness." F. B. Brightman (ed.), *Liturgies Eastern and Western* (Oxford: Clarendon Press, 1896), pp. 521, 535.

a common pattern began to appear for all preaching. It was marked by an introductory votum or a short prayer. Chrysostom usually began with the words: "Blessed be God. Peace be unto you," which were followed by a congregational response. To the same degree that prophecy definitely had become silent, the sermon had become the act of an office, primarily that of the bishop, who most often spoke sitting on his throne in the apse. He could also delegate the responsibility to the presbyters, who customarily made use of the ambos from which the texts were read. Sometimes Chrysostom and Augustine also spoke from the ambo. The service could become very long in an era when liturgy and sermon developed competitively; even Chrysostom sometimes saw the hearers leaving. At times, the church was empty by the time the believers' mass was to begin, after the sermon—it was the custom of Caesarius of Arles to command that the doors be kept shut!

Several factors contributed to the changed orientation of the sermon. The differentiation between the mass of the catechumens and the mass of the faithful began to be more sharply emphasized, and it was in this context that the need for catechetical preaching arose. Cyril of Jerusalem (c. 313-86) delivered his famous mystical catechetical addresses in the form of sermons. Origen's disciple, Dionysius of Alexandria, Gregory Thaumaturgus (St. Gregory of Neocaesarea) and Cyril of Alexandria delivered their exegetical expositions within the framework of the service. The fight against heresy was also to a great degree conducted from the pulpit.

But most significant of all was the fact that preaching inherited the legacy of ancient rhetoric, which now experienced its last great flowering. In our frame of reference rhetoric has a poor connotation. The people of antiquity, however, considered it one of the greatest forms of art. The rhetorical tradition permeates all Greek and Roman literature, and its formative influence on style was still apparent in an era when the art of speaking was in a period of decay. Education in late antiquity was rooted primarily in the schools of rhetoric. If the church was to speak in the language of the time to the masses which now rushed to meet her, she could hardly dispense with the aid that the schools of rhetoric had to offer. The danger involved was not hidden from the people of that day and again we are in the position of considering a secondary cultural motif. We have noticed how the diatribe shaped the pattern of earlier, less sophisticated preaching; now the panegyrical style also lived on in the sermon in the church. The dangers appear clearly in Eusebius' description of Paul of Samosata, who showed his pride even as a speaker: he beat his legs, stamped his feet and cursed those who did not express their appreciation, as they did in the theater, by waving and shouts of approbation (*Historia Ecclesiastica,* VII: 30).

During the fifth century the material which contributes to the history of preaching begins to grow tremendously in extensiveness. Hidden within this material are various critical problems, for example, those raised by the collection of mystical and ascetic homilies which earlier had been ascribed to Macarius the Elder, the Egyptian monk. The problems are by no means limited to the Greek language. The classicist of the Syrian Church, Ephraem Syrus, can also claim a place in the history of preaching. At least a few of the extant homilies and addresses of admonition which bear his name may be genuine. They are cast in poetic form and represent an intermediate form between preaching and religious poetry. The last great impulse, before the development reaches its height, is represented by the three Cappadocians, the brothers Basil the Great (c. 330-79) and Gregory of Nyssa (c. 330-c. 395), together with their friend, Gregory of Nazianzus (329-89) the most interesting personality of the three. We meet a bit of pulsating life, at the same time humanly appealing and strangely remote, in the writings of these men. The small episcopal cities in the interior of Asia Minor, where the name Christian has now been completely eradicated, once contained a humane and religious culture to waken our wonderment, and the extant literature gives us the opportunity of surveying its worlds both of the family and of spiritual work. Thus it is possible for us to discern the profiles of the various personalities.

The men and their work stand in bold relief against the double background of Julian's attempt to restore heathen antiquity and the tremendous crisis within the church which is usually called the Arian controversy. All three had come to the pulpit by way of the school of rhetoric. We observe in Greek rhetoric a contrast between two different lines of stylistic development: the pompous, heavy Asiatic style and the terse, disciplined, but rather pedantic Attic style. The latter designation especially, however, should be reserved for the exaggerated linguistic purism, which, in all respects, sets forth the Attic orators as the models of style. In this way the contrasting Asiatic style is seen as a less narrow classicism, as represented by the great contemporary teacher of rhetoric Libanius, Julian's and Chrysostom's teacher. We can also trace the same contrast in the art of Christian oratory. Asianism can be considered as represented by Gregory of Nazianzus, while Basil and Chrysostom are rather to be placed in the classical development. The art of Christian oratory may well be termed the final incarnation of the great rhetorical tradition of antiquity, but it could not be enclosed within its bounds. The dependence on the Bible was significant not only in furnishing the content but also in shaping the pattern of the proclamation. The rich imagery in the biblical prose has supplied a stylistic element in the Christian preachers' method of presentation which is lacking in the rhetorical art of their profane teachers, and this biblical prose was mediated to subsequent eras by these preachers.

The historic task of the Cappadocians was to unite the legacy of Origen with rhetorical training and Nicene orthodoxy. In their personal lives the sense of community contends with the powerful attraction of the ascetic life. This is source material for a historical drama which still awaits the creative hand of the artist. For us, the great Cappadocians must only be a stopping place along the way, even though this uncommonly fascinating area of study tempts us to delay. It is not possible to give a detailed analysis of their homiletical activity. Basil has left behind a series of sermons on the history of creation which have very often been plagiarized or imitated. An important source for our knowledge of ancient science, they also exhibit traits which remind us of the Enlightenment's speculations concerning the work of the Creator. From his pen we also have a series of homilies on the Psalms and a considerable number of addresses on various subjects without texts, most of them with an ethical-paranetic content. Four of Basil's eulogies on the martyrs belong in antiquity's panegyrical tradition of oratory but his ethical sermons continue to show dependence upon the diatribe. In the Cappadocians the rhetorical orientation tends to loosen the connection with the text: the literary sub-motif crowds out the exegetical element. The exposition of the text which is presented is, however, more sober than Origen's; Basil's exact understanding of the parables is a noteworthy example of this.

Gregory of Nyssa occupies a more important place in the history of dogma than in the history of preaching. His "great catechetical addresses" are hardly to be considered as homiletical productions. The allegorical method of interpretation, which he learned from Origen, is dominant in his biblical homilies. His extant addresses of consolation have, in a very detailed manner, been shown to be related to rhetorical patterns. A closer study of his homiletical production would uncover the beginnings of the textual sermon; the simple pattern of the homily has been abandoned and the sermon now moves in the direction of the synthetic method of a later era.

Gregory of Nazianzus occupies a unique place both personally and artistically. His varied career led from the bishop's palace in Cappadocian Nazianzus to the Byzantine patriarchal chair, from there back again to his home town, and last of all to the isolated life of an anchorite. A sensitive, egocentric, perhaps too emotional and anxious nature is exhibited in his writings, addresses, letters and poems, and above all in his autobiography, which is written in hexameter. To this we may add an occasional sign of sentimentality which most likely has its source in his Platonic world outlook. Few personalities in the ancient church appear before us in the same living way. Only one homily is found among the forty-five extant addresses, and we therefore lack the sources for evaluating Gregory as a textual expositor. In spite of its rhetorical technique, his eulogy in honor of the Maccabees is a conscious attempt to make the biblical characters emerge in their personal uniqueness. His festival sermons engage our interest most of all: here the exegetical element is wholly secondary but the theme of the festival is proclaimed with an almost ecstatic enthusiasm. These sermons may therefore be classed as having a liturgical character and may well be placed within the compass of the Eastern church's rich cult, as part of its developing liturgical texts. From Gregory's hand we also possess eulogies, in honor of the living and the dead, in both instances characterized by a lack of moderation which is repulsive from our modern viewpoint; we also possess a chastisement of Julian the Apostate, his former fellow student in Athens, characterized by violent invective which is equally repulsive. In his uncontrolled use of rhetorical flourish, antithesis, parallelism, rhyming articulation, and in the rushing flow of his short sentences, Gregory breaks the restraints of the classic art of oratory. In his most lofty outpourings he transcends the boundary between prose and poetry. In his history of Greek literature,

Wilamovitz-Moellendorff contrasts Gregory with the masters of the Attic art of oratory:

> Under the variegated mosaic and golden gleam of the Byzantine church's cupola, where the smoking oil lamps cast their light on the clouds of incense, this pathos is as much in order as the calm clear rational ethos of Pericles is on the naked Pnyx under Athens' open sky.[6]

We do notice in Gregory of Nazianzus, and also to some degree in the other Cappadocians, that the late Grecian rhetoric, coupled with the pattern of an Orientalism which is not Greek, acts as a violent flood to turn the Christian proclamation away from its proper furrow. This is an important and dangerous moment in the history of preaching. Here a closer investigation would be very much in order. Gregory of Nazianzus, as we know him, has hardly contributed toward a clearer understanding of the essential nature of Christian preaching; nonetheless, he is one of the most fascinating personalities in its annals.

Chrysostom

The Greek homily never rose to greater heights than it did in John, the Patriarch of Constantinople known subsequently to the world by the tasteless name Chrysostom, "golden mouth" (c. 337-407). The history of the ancient church does not present a more thrilling life story. To a higher degree than among the Cappadocians, all of the powers which shook the times are here interwoven in one man's tragic destiny. Here East and West, Hellenism and Christendom, asceticism and church order, flight from the world and court life, love and hate, ethical heroism and churchly political intrigue are all woven together in a color-

---

[6] Wilamovitz-Moellendorff, "Die griechische und lateinische Literatur, II, i," *Die Kultur der Gegenwart,* I, No. 7 (1912), 294.

ful kaleidoscope.[7] Original documents from this whole shifting history have been preserved, primarily a host of sermons and addresses on which the great crises, as well as the everyday, persevering service of the word, have left their imprint. Together with Savonarola and Luther, Chrysostom is one of the giant figures in the history of preaching: this is signified by no less extravagant an honor than Pius X's designation of him as the patron saint of preachers.

Born in the middle of the fourth century, the year of his birth being variously given, Chrysostom carried with him the impressions from a Christian mother's care. Set aside for the practice of law he became Libanius' student: it was the desire of the great rhetorician to have Chrysostom as his disciple. During this period of study he acquired his formal training in the art of speaking and this training remains the basic explanation for his technical competence and productivity as preacher. In addition, his spiritual awakening arose out of the ascetic movement of the time and its influence kept its hold on him throughout his whole life: the dualism between the life of contemplation which he sought and the active life which was thrust upon him was to a great degree determinative for his development. He was over thirty years old when he was baptized, after thorough preparation, and step by step he was drawn into the path of the preacher. As lector he became the student of Diodore of Tarsus and through him he was introduced to the earlier Antiochian scholarly tradition. Through Chrysostom this Antiochian tradition of realistic and exact biblical interpretation became a factor in the history of preaching and preserved him from the allurements of Origenism. Shortly thereafter he was called to the office of bishop; he declined and explained his motivation

---

[7] The most thorough presentation of the life and work of Chrysostom has been written by Chr. Baur, *Der heilige Chrysostomus und seine Zeit* (1929-30), Vol. I and II; the truly great biography is as yet unwritten.

in the essay "On the Priesthood": six years of life as a hermit had left their imprint on both body and soul. Socrates, the church historian, accused him of having some acidity in his temperament, which certainly was partly a result of the problems imposed by a poor digestion and a tendency to isolate himself. Both may have had a basis in the continuing allurement of the life of the hermit.

It was not until the year 381 that Chrysostom continued in the churchly path. Ordained as a presbyter in Antioch, he won there the reputation as preacher and counselor which became the occasion for his call in the year 397 to occupy the patriarchal chair in Constantinople. In this exposed position he grew to be a champion of righteousness, even as he experienced in rich measure the fickleness of court favor. Empress Eudokia's inconstancy, the hate of Eutropius the court eunuch, and the intrigues of opponents who were skillfully used by his rival for leadership in the church, Theophilus of Alexandria, filled the ten years in Constantinople with tensions, trials, and suffering. The hectic atmosphere in the half-Oriental world capital, political tensions in the nation and at court, dogmatic struggles, ecclesiastical political struggles are reflected in Chrysostom's addresses and sermons. The development reached its height in a double dethronement and exile. The first recall, after exile by the "Synod of the Oak" in 403, was made necessary by a disturbance among the lower classes, whom Chrysostom had previously captivated by his generosity as well as his eloquence. His second exile became final. He died in the year 407 in a faraway section of Pontus. Thirty years later his bones were triumphantly returned to the central city of the kingdom and his name was inscribed on the roll with other saints.

Chrysostom's literary production, which has survived the ravages of time, now consists of eight folio volumes. The main bulk consists of expository homilies: extant homilies are from Genesis (67 items), Psalms (60), Isaiah (6), Matthew (91),

John (87), Acts (55), Romans (32), I and II Corinthians (44 and 30), Ephesians (24), Philippians (15), Colossians (12), I and II Thessalonians (11 and 5), I and II Timothy (18 and 10), Titus (6), Philemon (3), and Hebrews (34). To this we may add homilies on isolated passages of Scripture. The boundary between homily and commentary is, as usual in the ancient church, by no means sharply drawn. Several series of homilies deal with a variety of subjects, such as the nine homilies concerning penance and the twelve against the antinomians, or they arise out of specific historical situations, such as the twenty-one homilies concerning the statues, delivered in Antioch in A.D. 387, when the statues of Caesar were torn down in a riot. A series of isolated homilies deal with other episodes in the eventful life of the preacher. Another group consists of eulogies in honor of the saints, including seven about the Apostle Paul, as well as other individual biblical characters. Sermons are also extant that deal with the great festivals of the church (Christmas, Epiphany, Good Friday, Easter, Ascension Day, Pentecost).

The most striking impressions one receives from the study of Chrysostom are the extensiveness of the production and the diligence of the preacher. Many of the homilies bear the marks of having been delivered day after day. The expository sermons were delivered at daily services during the week. Sometimes Chrysostom preached twice on the same day; he began the second homily "Concerning the Tempting Devil" with the statement that both his voice and his feet were exhausted by the address that he had delivered earlier, but the sight of the bishop who was present at the service now made him forget his fatigue. A few of his best-known homilies show some traces of having been delivered without preparation; an example is his address upon his return from the first exile. The person who usually regards unprepared presentations with a certain skepticism should recall the unusual background which was created by the rhetorical training of antiquity: the art of speaking itself has never been practiced with such enthusiasm or carried on with such skill as during this period of antiquity. Very likely, the addresses were most often prepared in written form. This, however, did not exclude extemporaneous digressions, which were not always an aid to coherence and organization. The sermons have generally been edited by stenographers and later revised and polished by the author himself.

The spoken word was a power such as it has seldom been in the history of the church, in this era when the liturgical service burst out in full and rich bloom. This certainly was partially due to the fact that the church's preachers were disciples of the rhetorical teachers and that many attended church in order to admire the practice of an art which was yet highly regarded. Chrysostom's attempts to restrain profane applause are well known, but they did not always succeed: we notice in an extant address how the art he employs in such an exhortation itself calls forth the applause which he sought to avoid. The addresses are, however, full of instances which show a lively contact between the speaker and his hearers. His whole career as a speaker contains many evidences that his preaching was a power both in the church and in the community and that his speeches were regarded as significant events.

Evaluations of Chrysostom's rhetorical gifts vary. Some have on occasion classified him as a true Atticist who continues the noblest tradition in Greek prose. On the other hand, his style often bears the marks of too many illustrations and of an undisciplined vocabulary placing him in clear opposition to the masters of Attic prose. His style has been influenced by the metaphorical language of the Bible. Although he surely cannot be regarded as an "Asian," his address nevertheless is extravagant, and introduction and digressions often claim too much emphasis. He uses and consciously changes the various stylistic arts. The diatribe often reappears in paranetic applications, in the use of short sentences and rhetorical questions which the author

35

himself answers. Chrysostom seems to consider the diatribe the natural form of the homily while in contrast, rhetoric plays the leading role in the panegyrical sermons on the saints and in the occasional addresses where the meaning of the text is not so important. The arrangement of the subject matter is hardly his greatest gift. The introductions, to which he gives special attention, claim too much space. Unity is often lacking. The exegetical homilies usually have two divisions: the first, a direct exposition of the text; the second, the application and admonition. At times, it seems as if his intractable gifts as a speaker violate all rules. The technical defects may be due to the fact that Chrysostom's literary legacy consists of actual addresses which are not the product of the writing table.

As we have already pointed out, the exegetical orientation appears strongly in Chrysostom's extant writings. The preacher sees his primary responsibility as the exposition of a text. The sermon has become commentary—perhaps due to the circumstance that the exegetical addresses have been more completely preserved than the others. The expository sermon did, however, continue the tradition of the Eastern church, especially the tradition from Origen. Even though Chrysostom by no means despises the allegorical method, it is, nevertheless, primarily his realistic Antiochian scriptural interpretation which has given him his prestige as the foremost biblical expositor among the church's preachers before the time of the Reformation. Jülicher's evaluation of his use of parables is especially well known: like no other expositor in ancient times, Chrysostom grasped the essential nature of parable and understood the difference between parable and allegory. Also, perhaps as no other before him, he made biblical characters live. His exposition of the Scripture has very nearly gained canonical status in the Eastern church.

The liturgical element is by no means lacking. A great many homilies must have been delivered at the Sunday mass, but the extant texts show only very insignificant traces of having been inserted into the liturgical context. The homilies in series were delivered at the daily services and we know very little about their ritualistic form. Information concerning the church sanctuary itself and particular incidents at the service are surely not absent, as in the case of the Antiochian sermons when he speaks of the presence of the bishop. Yet it is certainly significant that the liturgy has not left sharper traces in Chrysostom's preaching. We might rather say that it is very possible that the sermons tended to burst the bonds of the liturgical context because of their length and that the overpowering interest which is focussed on the spoken word must to some degree have made the cultic acts take second place. It is also very evident that the church year had little effect on the sermon. The church year shows its influence only in the addresses on festival days and in the Lenten sermons. These comments may, however, only claim provisional acceptance. It would be tremendously interesting to attempt a more careful investigation of the sermonic production of Chrysostom and other preachers of the early church from the liturgical standpoint.

If we define the prophetic element as an attempt, on the one hand, to actualize the gospel and, on the other hand, as the relation of the message to its environment and to present events, we will find rich source material in Chrysostom. His biblical exposition widens into an ethical paranesis which seeks to make the gospel live as a power for good works. In a sermon on alms he makes the penniless Christ appear and appeal in a way which is legitimate for all time. His moralism was by no means abstract since he attacked both the sins of the times and the sins of the hearers. His merciless precision in striking the right note was no minor factor in making enemies and bringing him distress. Protestant critics have found, in him and other Greek fathers, a touch of Pelagianism which sharply differentiates him from his great contemporary in the West, Augustine. These conclusions are based on Chrysostom's excessive glorification of ascetism and the life of the hermit as found especially in his early preaching.

On the whole it is impossible to modernize Chrysostom, yet it is patently a proof of his greatness that we are tempted to forget the distance which separates us. We find the distinctiveness of the Oriental character, the immersion in a culture and a type of Christianity which in spite of everything is far removed from contemporary man, more irritating in Chrysostom than in those fathers of the church who more clearly belong to a past era. One of the most fascinating facets of Chrysostom is that he stands squarely in his own time but simultaneously rises to a degree of timeless validity. As very few have been able to do, he made preaching an active force in the history of his own time and life. The Byzantine Empire with its variegated culture emerges very clearly in the many addresses which were delivered in specific historical situations. This is true of the Antiochian addresses concerning the statues, and especially true of the addresses which relate to the tragic crises of his own life. Here the addresses are complemented by extant letters which allow us to follow him during the days of his exile. All of the basic elements of the Christian sermon are to be found in this master of the Greek homily.

Powerful influences from other directions are also present in Chrysostom, above all, influences from the tradition of rhetoric. Chrysostom was aware of the dangers involved and at least sought to keep them within proper bounds. Nonetheless, his whole education had been shaped by the formal culture of the school of rhetoric. In his attempt to Christianize antiquity he still continued to be a child of antiquity much more than he himself realized. His treatment of the preacher's task as outlined in the essay "On the Priesthood" is a proof of this fact. Here the act of preaching is exalted; its difficulties are the main reason why the author has turned away from the exercise of the ministry. A specific strength of soul is required of the speaker, who must "tame the multitudes' undisciplined and dangerous desire for pleasure and make them listen with greater benefit, so that they allow themselves to listen and be led by him, and he is not led by their lusts." Natural gifts are necessary for this task, and labor also, and the labor becomes greater for him who has received a greater gift. Chrysostom's essay also exhibits the special difficulties of the time, when the masses, who had been only superficially influenced by Christendom as yet, streamed into the church and listened to the sermon, not with the mentality of disciples, but with the same critical superciliousness as the audience at a heathen play. It is when Chrysostom attempts to free the sermon from the shackles of rhetoric that the power of these shackles becomes apparent. In him we note the process by which preaching attempts to discover its own nature and gain clarity concerning its own essence. Sufficient time was not given, however, to reach the goal. The organic union of the exegetical, liturgical, and prophetic elements which would differentiate the sermon from the profane address Chrysostom introduced but did not actualize. The elements are there, but they have not been fused together.

The highest point in the history of the Grecian sermon also became its conclusion. This judgment may seem too harsh. Grecian sermons were also to be found subsequent to the time of Chrysostom. The Antiochian exposition of Scripture had a significant homiletical representative in Theodoret of Cyrrhus, albeit he followed his own inclinations in his sermons on the providence of God. On the other side, Cyril of Alexandria can claim a place in the history of preaching. The monks from the mountains of Syria and the deserts of Egypt also appeared as preachers, but they stifled the freshness of Christian preaching by unreal allegorizing and an exaltation of ascetic mysticism as the fulfillment of Christian piety. Eulogies on the mother of God and the saints supplanted expository preaching. The liturgical service increasingly became a mystical sacrifice in which the sermon could no longer retain its place. Preaching surely was not absent during the extended Middle Ages of the Greek church, in the various orthodox, heretical, and schismatic churches which spoke the Semitic and other Asiatic languages, nor in the more modern Eastern church. Here too, the traditional picture might be revised by more careful investigation, but we could hardly expect a radical re-evaluation.

THREE

Augustine and His Era

The Beginnings: Zeno and Ambrose

The beginnings of the Latin sermon are cloaked in obscurity. Greek, the language of the church during the early centuries, had at first been the language of preaching in the West. Hippolytus, the Roman church's greatest theologian at the beginning of the third century, still wrote and talked in Greek. To be sure, he was a schismatic, but the language did not play a significant role in his deviation. The rediscovery of a large part of Hippolytus' writings has not unearthed any new material for a history of preaching, for the addresses attributed to him are of disputed authenticity.[1] It is probable that his very extensive exegetical writings, many of which have been recovered, stem from homiletical addresses. This is, perhaps, less true of his commentary on Daniel than of his exposition of the Song of Solomon, which bears marks of a rhetorical orientation; for example, it mentions that Easter is imminent, as a sermon might do.

A Latin ecclesiastical literature arose first on African soil, Tertullian (c. 160-c. 220) being the first classic example. It is entirely possible that the great jurist of Christendom also preached; if so, his preaching must have shown traces of his rhetorical training. From the time of Tertullian on we must reckon with Latin rhetoric as a factor in the development of

---

[1] The address "Concerning the Holy Theophanies" has been defended as genuine by reputable scholars; see, for example, O. Bardenhewer, *Geschichte der Altkirchlichen Literatur* (2nd ed.; Freiburg: J. C. Herder, 1914), II, 600.

preaching in the West. He who wishes to do so may create an imaginative picture of Tertullian's method of speaking with the aid of his writings. The same restrained ardor, the same short, sentient, power-laden structure must have been characteristic of the speaker as of the author. We may also be sure that some of his writings originated as addresses. Nevertheless, we do not possess a single sermon from Tertullian.

We are in a somewhat better position when we consider the second of the great African fathers of the church, Cyprian. He, also, was a Christian rhetorician and his gifts as an orator were praised by Lactantius. Insofar as we are able to draw conclusions about his method of preaching from extant writings, we may be quite certain that a number of his tracts and hortatory writings originally had a homiletical character. We may say that in his use of the Bible, he applied the allegorical method only to a meager extent. He readily multiplied quotations from Scripture and related them to moral expositions, but sometimes these quotations were really meaningless. His presentation becomes more sharply colored as he describes the corruption which he attacks. As a man of action rather than thought, he develops with responsibility, and in times of danger and uncertainty he discovers the simple and sure word of faith which the situation demands.

Not until the fifth century do we meet more obvious sources for our study, and by the end of this century the Latin sermon reaches its absolute height in Augustine. This strange, sharp curve is to a degree explainable by the fact that we have lost the works of the older Latin preachers, but perhaps even more by the fact that the Greek influence acted as a restraining factor which required the powerful contribution of a creative genius before a breakthrough could be made. If we ignore Hilary of Poitiers, whose commentary may refer to homiletical expositions but from whom we possess no actual sermons there remain, only two names which attract our attention before the time of

Augustine: Zeno of Verona (d. c. 375) and Ambrose of Milan (c. 339-97).

Every visitor at Verona stands in wonderment before the exquisite basilica which bears Zeno's name. He has himself raised an interesting monument to himself in a collection of ninety-three tracts, most of which were originally sermons and are thus among the oldest examples of Latin preaching. They show the marks of a cultivated personality who stood at the zenith of the culture of his day and, not least, was acquainted with the classic literature of Rome. This also implies that he stood within the magic sphere of Latin rhetoric and shaped his prose in accordance with its patterns. This artistic skill, however, was limited to the method of expression since it was not accompanied by careful execution. A propensity for symbolic presentation is a part of his originality. Among the items he has preserved for us is the most complete description we own concerning the art of baking bread in antiquity. Specific sermonic texts are not given and the Bible is used superficially. Zeno's spiritual tracts also had a posthumous history even before they became the objects of modern, scientific critical scrutiny. According to the information given in the manuscripts, selected portions were used as addresses at the services of worship in Verona. Perhaps it is this circumstance which has rescued them from destruction. This also is a development which portends the beginning of the Middle Ages, when homiletical texts were very often adapted for liturgical usage.

The Greek influence is hardly less noticeable in Ambrose, the greatest personality of the northern Italian church in the fourth century. In his Confessions (VI:2, 3), Augustine testifies to the tremendous impression Ambrose made upon him. Augustine usually listened to Ambrose every Sunday in Milan, generally at high mass. This is one of the most interesting testimonies we possess from the ancient church concerning the influential power of the spoken word. We would hopefully have wished

Augustine to relate more about his great teacher's method of preaching, but the impressions from Ambrose were of interest to Augustine only to the degree that they influenced his own development. It is only incidentally that we have learned that Ambrose easily became hoarse and for this reason in his private studies usually read silently so as to save his voice. In his sermons to the people, Ambrose often returned to the word: "The letter kills, but the spirit gives life," using this verse to justify the biblical interpretations in which he "removed the mystical veil and spiritually opened the meaning" of offensive passages of Scripture.

In respect to Ambrose also we are only scantily provided with material for a primary investigation of his preaching. The ninety-nine extant homilies which bear his name are unanimously judged by the critics as spurious. These sermons are, nevertheless, not uninteresting examples of Latin preaching in the early church and therefore merit specific investigation. In addresses concerning his brother Satyrus, Caesar Valentinian II, and Theodosius I we meet a type of rhetoric which has little to contribute to Christian preaching. The book concerning the days of creation (*Hexaemeron*) was originally composed in a homiletical form and is basically a re-working of Basil the Great's renowned series of sermons on creation.

The main portion of Ambrose's homiletical legacy consists of his expositions of the Bible, such as the exposition of Psalm 119, and a commentary on the Gospel of Luke in which the original pattern of the sermon is still apparent. To this we may add a number of tracts on biblical and practical subjects. It was natural for the rhetorician and practically experienced public functionary, who through sudden elevation to the office of bishop became immersed in so many theoretical as well as practical problems, uncritically to adopt the legacy of Greek theology. This is also true in his dogmatic orientation, where he appeared as the champion of Nicene orthodoxy. Allegorical exegesis occurs less often in his writings than we would expect; the Scriptures played a significant role in his preaching and his treatment of the text is often characterized by a striking simplicity. Ambrose's sermons were constructed to a great degree on collated Scripture passages. For him the Bible was also of priceless value because more than anywhere else he could here find both a witness to the divine truths he always sought to espouse and a weapon against the evil powers which he tirelessly resisted. His pathos was basically ethically oriented. Though his dogmatic and ethical expositions were very weak, his presentation gained power and spirit when he was forced to give leadership in dangerous situations.

The pattern of Ambrose's preaching was given by the Roman rhetoric. Augustine's testimony concerning the irresistible power of attraction which this pulpit oratory by its *suavitas* could exert on a highly cultured young heretic makes us understand how great is the danger that in the modern evaluation of style and taste we depend upon the yardstick of a later time and treat the rhetorical production of the bygone era unfairly. From the information given by Augustine in the Confessions and substantiated by references in liturgical lections, references which editing has not removed, it is evident that Ambrose's preaching is set within the context of the service. Certain sections bear the marks of having been addressed to catechumens. It is reasonable to suppose that the father of Latin hymnody also directed his attention to the relationship between the spoken word and the liturgical context. It was the authority of Ambrose which succeeded in preserving remnants of the old Latin service in Milan, the service which was displaced in other locales by the Roman tradition. The Ambrosian liturgy belongs with the surviving sections of the pre-Roman service, usually grouped with it under the general designation of Gallican liturgy. When we take note in the text of the liturgy of the richly rhetorical style of prayer which was strongly influenced by Greek prototypes, we come to the conclusion that the Ambrosian pulpit oratory fits well into its liturgical context.

Augustine's Homiletical Activity

We do not possess a satisfactory monograph on the preaching of Augustine (354-430). His homiletical production does, however, present an uncommonly attractive task for research. The material is extensive and to a great degree it does leave the impression of being an accurate reflection of the oral proclamation. Here we meet one of the greatest personalities in the history of Christian thought as a diligent and passionate preacher. And here, for the first time, we see the Latin sermon shed the Greek yoke and assume an original form. This is one of the most significant crises in the annals of preaching. As we stand before this tremendous, incompletely investigated monument, the Augustinian sermons, we are sharply conscious how precarious it is to attempt to survey the development of Christian preaching.[2]

When, in the year 391, Augustine visited Hippo, he was prevailed upon by the people to accept the call as presbyter. By this decision he was torn away from the ascetic and contemplative life which he had chosen for himself, and was forced into an active career. It was not yet customary for a presbyter to

[2] Some of Augustine's sermons are available in English: *Nine Sermons of St. Augustine on the Psalms,* trans. Edmund Hill (New York: Kenedy, 1959); *Selected Easter Sermons of St. Augustine,* ed. Philip T. Weller (St. Louis: Herder, 1959); *Sermons for Christmas and Epiphany* (Westminster, Md.: Newman, 1952); *Sermones 1 to 50* (Newman, 1962); *Augustine: Later Works,* ed. John Burnaby ("Library of Christian Classics," Vol. VIII [Philadelphia: Westminster Press, 1955]), pp. 251-348, "Ten Homilies on the First Epistle General of St. John." Cf. also *Sermons on the Liturgical Seasons,* trans. M. S. Muldowny ("The Fathers of the Church," Vol. XXXVIII [New York: Fathers of the Church, Inc., 1959]), and *Ancient Christian Writers* (Newman, 1961), Vols. I-II. There are numerous sources in Latin, German, and French.

preach in the presence of a bishop, but the aging Bishop Valerius was anxious to receive Augustine's assistance in the task of preaching which normally rested upon the bishop himself. Augustine thus began to preach as a presbyter. His first sermon delivered during the Easter season 391 was most likely addressed to the catechumens in Hippo. In the background lay the whole development which is described in the Confessions; in the background lay rhetorical studies and extensive experience as a teacher in the art of oratory; in the background lay the inner development which had led him from his youthful life in Carthage to devotion to the ascetic ideal; in the background lay a restless pilgrimage of the spirit which had led him through Manicheism and Platonism to the Christian orthodoxy, as preached by Ambrose, which he now would begin energetically to espouse. The preacher at Hippo made use of all the elements in this experience. The greater part of Augustine's addresses were delivered in the little Numidian town which owes him its renown. A considerable number of these addresses do, however, preserve the memory of times when the great African father of the church was called to preach in Carthage or in other places.

The critics have identified as spurious some of the sermons which are extant under the name of Augustine. These pseudo-Augustinian sermons, which number more than three hundred, are by no means uninteresting. Even though they may not be used as sources for Augustine's own preaching they nevertheless bear witness to the influence which has emanated from him and they are interesting documents covering the extinct life of the ancient Latin church. In several instances there is naturally some doubt as to where we should draw the line between genuine and spurious material. That which has gained recognition as authentic certainly comprises one of the richest literary monuments we possess concerning the African church's culture, a culture which was obliterated in the conquest by the Vandals. The boundary between the actual sermons and the writings which have a homiletic origin is also very difficult to establish, as is usually the case. Under the category of sermons, three hundred sixty-three works are generally accepted as genuine. These are divided into various groups: sermons on texts from the Old and New Testament and sermons for the seasons of the church year, the homiletically more interesting group. The many festival sermons, both those on saints' days and those that deal with diverse subjects, belong in this latter category. But to these we must add several series on whole biblical books, such as the one hundred twenty-four treatises on John's Gospel, the ten homilies on the First Letter of John, and expositions on the Psalms which fill a thick folio volume, some of which retain traces of having been delivered as homilies. We must also consider a series of essays which are in reality re-worked addresses. Finally, later research has increased the extant heritage of genuine Augustinian sermons by several series of tens.

We thus have strong proofs of the industry with which Augustine practiced his office of teaching. At times he preached daily, especially in seasons of fasting; among the sermons for the seasons of the church year we have sermons for most of the holy days in the weeks between Quinquagesima and Easter. The connected biblical series must have been created by a continued day to day exposition: we have clear testimony that Augustine sometimes preached series which extended from three days to a week. Certain addresses served to instruct the catechumens and are mentioned as being directed to the catechumens (*ad catechumenos*) or to those about to be baptized (*ad competentes*). To a great extent the manuscripts of the addresses have been prepared from stenographic notes. In one instance Augustine improvised a sermon on an unexpected text when the lector by mistake read another Psalm than the one appointed for the day.

There are very few instances in the history of preaching where the extant manuscripts give us as vivid a picture of the oral sermon as we receive from the record of Augustine's sermons.

We notice the reaction of the hearers; preacher and congregation are in constant dialog. The lively African temperament shows itself in the applause, to which the speaker gives attention: "The words please you—I ask for good works." Even the reading of the text elicits comments that suggest participation on the part of the hearers. On one occasion the lesson from Matt. 11:25 was read and since the Latin used the word *confiteor* ("I thank thee"), the crowd, not understanding the context, beat their breasts as they usually did when they heard the word *confiteor* ("confess") in the confession of sin. The preacher used this incident as the occasion for his remarks. A few of the extant sermons are followed by communications in the form of announcements to the congregation. Augustine personally dictated or wrote some of his sermons; less often, he used a written and memorized rough draft. Under no circumstance was he bound to the written word. He did have the opportunity of tangibly witnessing the power of the living word, as when he succeeded in abolishing a popular barbaric custom in Mauretanian Caesarea—he knew that he had touched the hearts of his hearers when he saw tears in their eyes. Augustine usually called his hearers *caritas vestra*—literally, "your love"; it was as if he had made a polite greeting of his own theological idea of love. To be sure, he also experienced occasions when few attended church, yet we do gain the general impression that the hearers' willingness to listen greatly stimulated his zeal as a preacher.

Rhetoric and the Sermon

Augustine's relation to the rhetorical tradition to which he belonged is an interesting question. Probably he stood in a dialectical relation to it: he consciously sought to emancipate the churchly proclamation from the techniques of profane oratory and at the same time he continued to be a rhetorician and contributed to the continued influence of ancient rhetoric on the history of preaching. The fourth book in the essay *De Doctrina Christiana,* which is usually characterized as the first attempt to write a homiletics, is the classic original document on the relation between rhetoric and preaching. While the first book gives the basic conceptual analysis of the relation between thing (*res*) and sign (*signa*), the religious reality and its concrete manifestation, and the two following books contain biblical hermeneutics, a summary of the principles of biblical interpretation, the fourth attempts to impart rules for the art of the spiritual address. The book proves that Augustine believed that the sermon was basically the exposition of a text and he did place spiritual rhetoric within the framework of this context. This fourth book was written much later than the others, toward the end of the author's life, and may therefore claim to be the result of the experiences of a lifetime.

If in this essay by Augustine we expect to find practical guidance for the inexperienced in the art of preaching, we will be deeply disappointed. Here the presentation revolves around the orbit of basic principles. Many edifying instructions are given to the preacher who, in the school of the Spirit, wishes rightly to benefit his hearers. He shall seek God's guidance in prayer so that he receives his message from above. He must always make the quality of the content and the welfare of the hearers more important than the outward form. The wise speaker is greater than the orator; his greatest desire is to be understood. Augustine now takes great pains to show that the biblical authors have their own rhetoric which does not lack for parallels in the methods of embellishment and the figures which profane oratory uses. Nevertheless oratory is here presented as the humble servant of wisdom. Augustine explains his thesis by using interesting examples from Amos and the letters of Paul. More significant, however, for the history of the art of preaching, is the fact that Augustine in this essay applies the rules of classical rhetoric concerning the purpose of the address and the use of various styles of presentation. It is through his influence that later homileticians began to follow Cicero. He advocates the well-known definition of the task of the speaker: *docere* ("teach"), *delectare* ("delight"), and *flectere* ("influence"), in order to be able to appeal to intellect, feeling, and will. Furthermore, he explains carefully how the speaker shall make use of the three styles of address: *genus submissum, temperatum,* and *grande* ("the restrained, the moderate, and the grand style"). Many of his practical proposals have not lost their validity, especially his reminder that an audience will no longer tolerate the use of the grand style of speaking. He also gives advice worth considering about the beauty of the artless, and about the special charm of the restrained style where expression becomes the complete servant of the subject and the form reflects the content. The three styles have each their own purpose, and these purposes correspond to the aims of oratory. Each shall make its contribution so that the address is received *intelligenter* ("intelligently"), *libenter* ("willingly"), and *obedienter* ("obediently"). The grand style shall serve to influence the will and to evoke obedience. The life of the preacher is, however, the most effective, sublime speech.

It would be interesting to study the application of these rules in Augustine's own sermons. It is evident that the trained rhetorician seriously and consciously sought to achieve simplicity and intelligibility. The reader is constantly grasped by the spirit of the short sentences, by the fiery temperament which seems to make the sentences chase each other, and by the enhanced intensity evoked by questions and exclamations. Even though Augustine clearly and purposefully avoids the artistic period, he by no means despises other methods of embellishment such as parallel expressions and rhyming sentence endings. He has a striking weakness for pointed word combinations and plays on words. He leaves a peculiar impression in the conclusion of an address to the newly baptized delivered on Easter Sunday (*ad populum et ad infantes, seu eodem die baptizatos*). The sermon warns against adultery and concludes with a call to repentance:

> When are you going to reform? When are you going to change? "Tomorrow," you say. Behold, how often you say: "tomorrow, tomorrow"; you have really become a crow.[3] Behold, I say to you that when you make the noise of a crow, ruin is threatening you. For that crow whose cawing you imitate went forth from the ark and did not return. Instead, my brother, return to the church, which the ark then represented. O you who are newly baptized, hear me; you who have been re-born through the blood of Christ, hear me. I beg you by the name which has been invoked upon you, by the altar to which you have approached, by the sacraments which you have received, by the future judgment of the living and the dead, I beg you, I put you under obligation in the name of Christ, not to imitate those persons who you know are such as I described. On the contrary may the sacraments of him who did not wish to come down from the cross, but who did wish to rise from the tomb endure.[4]

He speaks the living African Latin used by his congregation, and he is well aware of the divergence from classical usage. Sometimes, especially in his holiday sermons, he rises from the simple exposition to a rapturous artistry which transcends the boundary between poetry and prose, on occasion reminding us of the sequences of style in the church of the Middle Ages. These oratorical passages of splendor, where the grand style flourishes, certainly are more effective addressed to the ear than to the will. They lend themselves better to quotation than to

---

[3] Cf. Gen. 8:7. The words "tomorrow, tomorrow," in Latin, *cras, cras,* approximate the cawing of a crow.

[4] Quoted from "The Fathers of the Church," Vol. XVII, New York, 1959, Sermon 224, p. 188.

translation.[5] They may give the impression of an empty display of words, but the contrast of rhyming phrases corresponds to the dialectic of the theological thought.

The arrangement of the subject matter is strikingly simple; often it is wholly absent. Augustine avoids the elaborate, often somewhat extended introductions which the Greek preachers loved. The introduction is usually characterized by a studied simplicity although there are significant exceptions to this rule. The speaker generally relates himself to the lection from Scripture which he has chosen as a text and sometimes gives a short recapitulation of an earlier sermon, especially when he is dealing with a series of expositions. Sometimes he recalls that he has given a promise to deal with a specific subject. Otherwise it is exceptional that he announces a theme, as here:

> Through the apostle the truth calls us to bear one another's burdens, and just through this to which he calls us, namely that we bear each other's burdens, he also shows us, what fruit comes from it, since he appends a word and says: then you fulfill the law of Christ. This law is not fulfilled unless we bear each other's burdens. With the help of God I will try to show, which these burdens are and how they must be borne, since with all our powers we must seek to fulfill the law of Christ.[6]

[5] One of Augustine's Nativity sermons contains the following prose hymn: "In the bosom of his Father, He existed before all the cycles of ages; born of an earthly mother, he entered upon the course of the years on this day. The Maker of man became man that he, Ruler of the stars, might be nourished at the breast; that he, the Bread, might be hungry; that he, the Fountain, might thirst; that he, the Light, might sleep; that he, the Way, might be wearied by the journey; that he, the Truth, might be accused by false witness; that he, the Judge of the living and the dead, might be brought to trial by a mortal judge; that he, Justice, might be condemned by the unjust; that he, Discipline, might be scourged with whips; that he, the Grape, might be crowned with thorns; that he, the Foundation, might be suspended upon a cross, that Courage might be weakened; that Security might be wounded; that Life might die." (From *ibid.*, Sermon 191, p. 28.)

[6] [Augustine, Sermon 164; translated from Brilioth's rendering.—TRANSLATOR.]

53

Even though Augustine generally tries to keep a certain unity in his addresses, he sometimes departs from this rule and delivers sermons on very disparate subjects and passages of Scripture. A clearly given outline is even more rare than a specific theme. An address on penance does, however, contain three divisions and speaks first concerning the baptism which precedes, second concerning daily penance, and third concerning the penance which refers to special mortal sins. A sermon on the good shepherd is divided according to the category of persons: the shepherd, the hireling, the thief. Augustine's sermons do give the specific impression of being spontaneous outpourings where the preacher speaks that which comes to mind and then unexpectedly stops when it seems to be enough. Yet this artlessness is itself often a carefully hidden art.

Augustine intentionally sought to address people. The formal shortcomings are surely a testimony to the fact that we have real, living addresses before us and not the product of the writing table, even though his sermons usually show the marks of careful preparation. This is especially true of the purely exegetical homilies. He could end very arbitrarily and leave the conclusion for another day. "I believe I have talked long enough," he says in one sermon, "but, nevertheless, I have not come to the end of the Gospel lection. If I should complete the rest, I would tire you, and I fear, that what you have learned would be lost: therefore this must be enough for *caritas vestra* ('your love'). We are not stewards only now, but so long as we live, and we live for your sakes." A homily on Psalm 72 ends with these words: "I have forgotten how long I have been speaking. The Psalm is ended and I attribute my perspiration to the fact that I have delivered a long address, but I cannot do enough to answer your enthusiasm. You have a violent effect upon me. Ah, if you only showed the same enthusiasm in grasping the kingdom of heaven." As a general rule the sermons were conspicuously short; some extended not more than a period of ten minutes, although others used up a half hour. Sometimes when they assume the form of more extensive treatises it is apparent that we do not have the oral address before us, but a later redaction. A sermon for the season of Epiphany (First Sunday after Epiphany) ends with the words: "It is meet that an old man's address should not only be serious but also short." Augustine seems to have developed the art of ending unexpectedly, but also with a powerful final chord which must have echoed in the ears of his hearers. Often he uses only a word of Scripture followed by a doxology or a liturgical prayer.

Exegesis

It is evident that as a preacher Augustine wished to be a scriptural expositor. In this respect he agreed with his Greek predecessors and contemporaries. We have already mentioned that he set forth the oratory of the biblical writers as a pattern for the preacher in his *De Doctrina Christiana*. A great part of his extant homiletical production consists of continued commentaries on John's Gospel and the Psalms. His sermons for the seasons of the church year relate to biblical texts and sometimes are interwoven with allusions to personalities and words of Scripture. Augustine's whole homiletical production is replete with biblical material, but it hardly bears the imprint of biblical simplicity.

An investigation of Augustine's place in a history of biblical exposition would require careful study in the form of an inquiry into his application of the principles enunciated in *De Doctrina Christiana*.

Exegetical development in the ancient church reaches its conclusion in Augustine. Doubtless, he was always anxious to establish literal and essential meaning, which he sought to apply whenever it had devotional value.[7] Allegorizing, however, was a self-evident alternative to Augustine, since the practice of lecturing on the whole Bible gave him, as well as other preachers in the ancient church, the responsibility of exegeting texts less devotional—even indifferent. For posterity, it is difficult to judge this practice with complete fairness, since we cannot recapture an understanding of Scripture whereby historical perspective was lacking; all things were of a single category or, at most, divided into the Old and the New Testament; and every line was read as containing a divine truth. To Augustine, that truth was his doctrine of love. Although Augustine did not wholly lack a historical understanding of the Old Testament personalities as messengers and precursors, his view of Scripture was controlled by the typological outlook, "The New Testament is concealed in the Old: the Old is revealed in the New." Everything related in Scripture about Abraham is simultaneously history and prophecy. Augustine is not alone in finding support for the allegorical method in the passage from Galatians (4:22 ff.) concerning the two sons of Abraham, which signify the two covenants. That interpretation was never questioned in his time, for Origen had been the exegetical instructor for all antiquity; compared to him, the great Latin father is measured and sober. Augustine's own thoughts on *res* and *signa* lend themselves well to subtle discussions of the tropological and enigmatic character of obscure passages of Scripture. Augustine, moreover, by no means limited the allegorical interpretation to the types of the old covenant. An example of a similarly outrageous use of a New Testament story is the explanation given the wedding in Cana, a passage which has always suffered at the hands of expositors. Sometimes Augustine lost himself in the

[7] Jülicher places Augustine ahead of Jerome in reference to their ability to exegete parables. Augustine, however, in common with the other exegetes of the ancient church, did not understand the difference between parable and allegory. A. Jülicher, *Die Gleichnisreden Jesu* (2nd ed., 1910), pp. 243-44.

strangest type of mystical address. At the same time he possessed an understanding of the central biblical concept so brilliant that it brought him deeper into the world of the Bible than any of his predecessors. This spiritual affinity perhaps appears most clearly in his treatment of John's Gospel.

When a Catholic historian,[8] writing in our time on the history of preaching, claims that homiletic exegesis has never progressed beyond Augustine, he may testify to his own limited viewpoint, but he also gives a well-deserved compliment to the greatest preacher of ancient times. Nevertheless, as a textual expositor, Augustine cannot be placed ahead of the great Antiochian in the patriarchal see at Constantinople.

Liturgical and Prophetic Elements

In the previous presentation, we have caught a glimpse of the liturgical elements in Augustine's preaching. In countless instances he began with a reminder of the lections to which the congregation had listened a few moments earlier. No fixed order of pericopes was yet established, but the choice of texts was limited by consideration for the festivals of the church year. In Augustine we can see how these texts began to grow together into a prescribed order.

The liturgical influence appears strongly in the subjects for the Lenten season. Here as early as in Augustine, we discover a tradition which has survived through the centuries. The Lenten days were above all others and were celebrated by a daily preaching which bore the imprint of the spirit of repentance. The Cross was the basic motive for fasting, self-denial, and good works. We constantly find Lent held up as the catechumens' specific season of preparation for the great bap-

[8] F. Stingeder, *Geschichte der Schriftpredigt* (1920), p. 50.

tismal festival. Augustine thus speaks on Palm Sunday on the transmission of the confessions of faith. During Holy Week he preaches on the re-presentation of the confessions of faith with special attention to the higher division of catechumens about to be baptized. His oratorical gifts appear in full flower on Easter Sunday: his artistry appears in the humble confession (of a practiced rhetorician) that his lips could not utter what he had understood, that his tongue could not correctly interpret the joy of his heart. Preaching every day of the week following Easter, he used the occasion to continue the instruction of the newly baptized. He did not ignore either the Emmaus disciples, treated even at this time on Monday, or the doubting Thomas, considered then, as now, on the Sunday after Easter. The Day of the Ascension of Our Lord gave him the opportunity to emphasize that faith must proceed from the seen to the unseen. Pentecost, which also appears to have been a baptismal festival, had a similar message: the Spirit could not come while the disciples were dependent on the Lord's bodily presence. Christmas had not yet gained parity with the older festivals, yet its theme awakened a special resonance in Augustine, who loved to preach on the miracle of the virgin birth as well as that of the incarnation. We possess some thirteen Christmas sermons. Epiphany also, even though it was a newcomer from the Orient, gave the preacher in Hippo an opportunity to speak on subjects dear to his heart. Among the various subjects which have contended for consideration on this day, the star of the East and the firstborn among the Gentiles began to assume their customary place. Epiphany was already a day of missions for Augustine. It is especially captivating to notice how the familiar rhythm of the church year begins to take shape in one of the church's greatest preachers and how this rhythm shows its influence both in stimulating preaching and in giving variety to the message. Among the liturgical sermons we can also include the numerous sermons on the saints as well as the homilies delivered on special holidays, for example, on the anniversary of the dedication of a church or at the dedication of an altar.

The striking brevity which often marks Augustine's preaching is essentially due to the sermon's place in the cult. This position has also frequently left its influence on the content of the sermon. Sometimes we find a short summary of all three lections; their striking correspondence on occasion gives the speaker his subject. One sermon begin with the words: "The Gospel lection recently sounded in our ears." Sometimes we meet allusions to other sections of the liturgy. Thus the preacher reminds us, in a sermon on one of the Sundays after Epiphany, of the beginning of the liturgy of the Lord's Supper. When the preacher says, "Lift up your hearts," the faithful answer with assurance, "We lift them up unto the Lord." This is combined with the words of the apostle, "For our conversation is in heaven," [9] and the application is made, "If consequently the conversation of the faithful is in heaven, since they possess the true love, then the root of love is planted in heaven." It is evident that for Augustine preaching was an essential part of the service. Its uniqueness derived from its relationship to the liturgy.

No worthier representative of the prophetic office appeared in the history of the church before the time of the Reformation than the Bishop of Hippo. Few others have spoken a word in a specific situation that has attained universal significance and retained its actuality after centuries. His addresses surely do not, like those of Chrysostom, bear the imprint of having been created in dramatic situations filled with tension; nonetheless, his great, lifelong struggle against both Manicheans and Donatists did leave clear traces in his sermons. Many of the sermons can barely be described as general declarations. The living dialog between speaker and hearer, of which we have

---

[9] Phil. 3:20 in the Authorized Version uses the word "conversation." This translation corresponds to Augustine's use of the Latin word *conversatio.*

already given examples, is proof that the sermons were addressed to a specific community. Moral exhortations, which were strongly emphasized in the preaching of the Western church, did not gain prominent status in the Augustinian sermon—moralizing is generally better suited to Pelagians than to preachers of an extreme theology of grace. Nevertheless, Augustine's sermons by no means lack ethical urgency, even if that urgency is somewhat onesidedly aimed at unchastity and adultery. Above all else, however, Augustine conceived of himself as a steward of the mysteries of God. The classic Augustinian representations of love and of the humble Christ are often repeated. The practical, popular sermons are vessels filled with precious drink, the deepest and most intimate theological thoughts of ancient times, many of which have neither gone out of date nor lost their power to captivate. In those sermons we meet some of the classic aphorisms Augustine so enjoyed.[10] A presentation of the contents of Augustine's sermons would also become an analysis of the Augustinian theology. Here the historian of preaching must, as always, exercise care lest he merely supply a compendium of dogma. Instead we must fasten our attention on the work of preaching which gave theological labor a living form and made it a factor in the contemporary worship of the congregation.

Nowhere have we met the three basic elements of the sermon in such balance and with such creative reciprocal action as in Augustine. It is also true that in him the sermon has begun to find its own pattern. The rhetorical tradition, still evident, is no longer a shackle. A new pattern has begun to emerge, although it has not yet gained full stability. A real understanding of inner unity and logical order are especially lacking. Such elements often are, however, of a secondary importance to a creative genius. Preaching which is full to the brim with con-

---

[10] See Sermon 188: "Human pride brought you to such a depth that only divine humility could raise you up again." (From "The Fathers of the Church." Vol. XVII, p. 19.)

tent, which foams with prophetic urgency, can afford to neglect the instrumentalities which lesser spirits need if they are not to fail utterly. One of the marks of spiritually impoverished times is too great a concern for external form. It will also become apparent, however, that the rhetorical task is by no means unimportant.

The Latin Sermon after Augustine

After the time of Augustine, the ancient Latin sermon lost its power. Both late antiquity and the Middle Ages depended upon the Bishop of Hippo's legacy and they often sought to hide their poverty under his mantle. Preaching in the Western church, nevertheless, retained more life and power in the centuries immediately following Augustine than preaching in the Eastern church had after the time of Chrysostom. New developments were not absent, especially the contribution of Greek theology and the ideal of monasticism's ascetic life, mediated first of all by Jerome, who also by virtue of his industry as a biblical expositor deserves a place in the annals of preaching. Otherwise, however, the expository homily is forced into the background. Augustine in his time could still prescribe his own lections at the service, but as the church year gained a more established form, the appointment of pericopes became more rigid. The sermon on Sunday became an exposition of the Gospel for the day. The liturgical context began to be more tightly closed. By degrees the sermon was cramped within the boundaries drawn as a result of the luxuriant flowering of the cultic forms.

As we move from Augustine to Leo the Great (d. 461), the greatest Roman bishop of the fifth century, we notice some continuity, but more discontinuity. Here the sources are more scanty. The ninety-six sermons extant are much more limited in their scope than Augustine's. Leo had a remarkable interest in celebrating his own anniversaries: we have sermons on the anniversaries of his ordination and of his elevation to the episcopal see of Rome. Besides these, the collection contains a series of festival sermons, Christmas and Epiphany being especially well represented. The Passion season, particularly Holy Week and especially Wednesday in Holy Week, is more richly represented than Easter or Pentecost. Preaching had already at this time assumed a particular pattern during seasons of fasting to which Leo's homiletical legacy bears testimony: nine sermons extant belong to the December fast (Advent), twelve to the season of Lent, four to the Ember days in September. Peter's, Paul's, and other Roman saints' days gave Leo the opportunity to express himself. The sermons on the collects are unusual.

Leo's preaching is more distinguished by the luster of his style than by the depth of his content. He is concerned lest he tire his hearers by long speeches; on one occasion he ends rather abruptly, saying he fears to lose the attention of his hearers. Roman authors see Leo's sermons as the model for the majestic and polished style which was later used by the incumbents of Saint Peter's throne. He loves antithesis and original stylizations and enthusiastically embellishes his addresses with rhetorical flourishes. This attention to the outer garment also expresses itself in assonance and rhythmical cadences. The *cursus leoninus,* his balanced prose rhythm, became normative for the style of the Roman curia and also set its stamp on the construction of the Roman collects.

Leo preached a completed faith where nothing was to be added and nothing subtracted—a dogmatic fortress to be defended against the unfaithful. For his own time, this meant particularly the defense of the formula of Chalcedon's doctrine concerning the two natures in opposition to the Monophysites. Pure doctrine, for Leo, had its primary significance in its power to create good works. He reinterpreted the legacy from Augustine in a moralistic way, adding contributions from the

Orient. He gave the fight against the demons primary emphasis: we must take our stand against the devil and his followers.

We find the same characteristics in Leo's contemporary, Peter Chrysologus ("golden word"), Metropolitan of Ravenna. His extant addresses, numbering one hundred seventy-six, are a different sort of monument to the former greatness of Ravenna than the city's famed mosaics, even though they cannot compete with the mosaics' abiding splendor. In content, these addresses may be classed as average examples of the Latin sermon. Ravenna was certainly more accessible to influences from the Orient than other areas in the western half of the Empire and such influences are evident in the ostentatious rhetoric which makes Peter Chrysologus' preaching unappetizing to contemporary readers. Nevertheless, Peter's surname does bear witness to the regard his preaching enjoyed in his own time as well as in a much later era, especially the period of French Neoclassicism. From him we possess a series of Sunday and holiday sermons probably delivered on prescribed pericopes. He uses the Bible superficially and often ruins the most simple biblical narratives by arbitrary allegorizing. He makes the parable of the prodigal son deal entirely with the Gentiles (the lost son) and the Jews (the elder brother). The church year and the cult exercised a decisive influence. Remarkably enough, he did not preach during Holy Week; he explains in a sermon on Easter Sunday that the toil of the vigils and the fatigue brought on by the fasts constrained him to refrain. He also suspended his preaching during a period of intense heat. The discipline of the catechumens appears in several sermons. It is yet customary to excuse the catechumens when the mass of the faithful begins. The aim of the sermon is primarily ethical: it must discourage sin and encourage good works. This was the basic theme of preaching in late antiquity and continued to be the theme during the Middle Ages.

We discover the same tendencies in one of Peter Chrysologus' contemporaries, the Italian preacher Maximus of Turin. Like Peter, Maximus had a classical Greek orientation, but he was less affected. His sermons are of greater interest to the history of culture than to the history of preaching, since they show how the twilight of culture shadowed the Latin church even before the church could conquer the native heathendom. We hear about the worship of Diana, about the popular frolic at New Year's— a practice which has always been a matter of concern for preachers—and about the superstitions connected with the eclipse of the moon, a motif which reappears in the preaching of the early Middle Ages. The church saw eclipses more rationally than the popular notion that the moon needed the help of song and all kinds of noise to overcome the monster which seemed to be devouring it.

The Italian preachers apparently had little regard for their inheritance from Augustine; his tradition did continue in Christian Gaul to influence the spiritual life of the early Middle Ages. Caesarius of Arles (d. 542) was the most important intermediary. Untiringly, he defended the churchly legacy from antiquity and made it accessible in the midst of the confusion of mass migrations. As Metropolitan of Arles, which next to Rome was the most important churchly center in the West, he advocated the improvement of worship life. Laymen were allowed to sing hymns and liturgical responses and also to learn the Creed and the Our Father. Preaching was, however, an unforfeitable element in the service. A synod in southern Gaul emphasized the priest's responsibility to preach, a most significant development in contrast to the period when it was considered a real sensation for a presbyter to preach in the presence of a bishop. A deacon was to read a homily from the writings of the Fathers if the priest could not be present. In the large dioceses north of the Alps, the parish priest was given a more independent status. During his forty years of service as bishop, Caesarius, as one of his aims, consciously followed the policy of fortifying the tradition which made preaching a necessary element in the service. Protestant presentations have, perhaps, had a tendency to idolize Caesarius, in contrast to the altogether too Roman Gregory the Great, and to make the ascetic hierarch, who was wholly controlled by the monastic ideal, the exponent of the pure gospel in a dark age.

The most interesting facts about Caesarius are on the one hand his indomitable interest in the task of preaching itself, which he promoted both by word and deed, and on the other hand his dependence on Augustine, which caused a large share of his own homiletical production to be placed among the pseudo-Augustinian sermons. It is a difficult critical task to sort out the genuine material, a task which remains uncompleted. Caesarius is certainly worthy of honor and remembrance because of his enthusiasm for the word of God. One of the pseudo-Augustinian sermons, of which Caesarius is most certainly the author, states that the word should not be honored less than the body of God, a likely reference to the word that is read. He was himself a tireless preacher and he gladly furnished sermon manuscripts to his weaker brethren. He was by no means a stranger to the art of using borrowed materials. Preaching was in the process of becoming a mechanical trade. The unoriginal compilation was often the only kind of literary production of which the times were capable. Caesarius, however, had the gift of speaking the language of the people and of appealing to the imagination of his hearers in descriptive pictures. His originality lay in this gift; the message itself came from Augustine. Thus Caesarius was saved, in spite of his enthusiasm for asceticism and the monastic ideal, from the moralistic superficiality which characterized so many of his contemporaries. He had learned from Augustine that love of God is the source of good works.

Not the Gallic Metropolitan but a Roman bishop, however, became the foremost intermediary between antiquity and the Middle Ages. Gregory the Great (d. 604) was an ascetic in the same sense as Caesarius. The call to active duty came to him, as it came to Gregory of Nazianzus and Chrysostom, as an outward compulsion. Love for the quietness of contemplation never left him, but practical tasks made his gifts as a leader of men and a hierarch evident. In his *Liber Regulae Pastoralis,* which became the classic source for pastoral theology in the Roman church, he contributed a western counterpart to Chrysostom's essay concerning the office of the ministry. Some homiletical directions are given, but the essay is basically concerned with the task of the care of souls. Gregory is known as a diligent preacher but his extant sermons are relatively few in number: twenty-two homilies on Ezekiel, delivered in the year 593 when the Lombards attacked Rome, together with forty homilies on the Gospel lessons prescribed in the mass, which surely derive from his first year as Bishop of Rome (590). We know, furthermore, that he delivered homilies on several books of the Bible. His much-read commentary on the Book of Job had its genesis in lectures before a group of monks, and sections of it were delivered later at services in some churches. We have unusually clear information as to how the extant manuscripts were produced: They were edited by use of stenographic notes, although a considerable number of the homilies for Sundays were dictated by Gregory but delivered by others when he was ill. He suffered from a disease of the stomach and also had a disease of the throat which made it difficult for him to be heard. A sermon delivered in the Basilica of the Holy Virgin on Easter Sunday began with the information that he had been unable to deliver his own sermons; since he had noticed that this had affected the attention of the hearers adversely, he now required of himself, "within the solemn context of the mass, to interpret the Gospel lection, not by means of dictation, but through speaking." The spoken word should grasp the hearers like a solicitous hand—*quasi quadam manu sollicitudinis.*

Gregory's preaching leaves a poor impression in contrast to

that of Augustine or even of Leo the Great. It has little of the formal elegance which characterized his predecessors, and the sweep of thought which characterizes Augustine is entirely lacking. The eclipse of the Latin sermon has to a degree been conditioned by the decayed state of rhetorical training. Gregory interprets his pericopes, which seem to have become solidly established, somewhat tritely; the texts themselves have been inserted in the written manuscript. First of all, he seeks to extract the ethical motifs from Scripture; his means is an unspiritual play on the "hidden meaning," an allegorizing, which very often dissipates the real content. No spirit of prophecy is found here, even though Gregory is anxious to present the demands of the times to his audience and his paraneses are sometimes characterized by the real warmth and seriousness of the shepherd of souls. The cultural decline he seeks to combat has settled upon his own world of thought. If the naive superstition which is discussed in his dialogs "concerning the lives and miracles of the Italian Fathers" (*De Vita et Miraculis Patrum Italicorum*) has not left any traces in his sermons, they are still typical of the general atmosphere of the time.

Gregory, the organizer of the Roman cult who more than any other man influenced the order of the mass which was to supplant all other orders in the Latin West, was just as anxious as anyone that the sermon should retain its place in the mass. His good example at this point is, perhaps, his primary significance in the history of homiletics. In spite of everything, the demand for preaching within the solemn context of the mass—*inter missarum sollemnia*—was never ignored in the Roman church of the Middle Ages; yet the solicitude for the cult itself, to which Gregory contributed mightily, became the chief enemy of preaching in the Roman church. Gregory was no stranger to the practice of reading at mass a homily from an acknowledged teacher of the church. The custom unfortunately won a fixed place in the prayer offices, and passages from the homilies of the fathers are even today a part of the Roman breviary. The practice indicated that the liturgy had smothered the sermon, making it a mere section of liturgy, which could only happen in an era when exposition of Scripture had dried up and when the spirit of prophecy had departed from the church.

FOUR

The Middle Ages

The Carolingian Renaissance

In various realms of historical scholarship we may speak of a rediscovery of the epoch which, in spite of all objections, we must continue to call the Middle Ages. This is true not least in the annals of preaching. Within this period we must differentiate a basically reproductive period from a more independently creative era. The boundaries may be variously established but the twelfth century is the line of demarcation. The homiletical material extant from before 1100 is not insignificant, but if we seek original contributions of lasting value, we will find that the field is radically restricted before that date.

In the centuries of their dominance, the German missions were not able to extend themselves further in their preaching than to mediate to the new peoples chosen fragments of the inheritance from the ancient church. The preacher became primarily a translator whose task was to transfer the homilies of the Fathers into the Romance or German folk languages. Samples of this activity which have come to our attention are few and of doubtful authenticity. Thus sermons which earlier were attributed to SS. Columba and Boniface have been rejected by historical criticism. The earliest preserved traces of sermons in the folk languages belong to later centuries. Artless interpretation and a clumsy mode of expression to some degree give these homiletical productions the character of simple primitiveness. Here we are reminded of the Anglo-Saxon homilies of Aelfric the Grammarian, which surely are a hundred years older than the earliest German collections. In Gaul, the Latin culture persevered longer than in other sections north of the Alps, but even here the necessity of preaching in the language of the people soon arose, Latin continuing only as the language of literature. Throughout the Middle Ages, clerics continued the custom of making their sermon outlines in Latin, even though they spoke French or German.

The Carolingian Renaissance gave new life to the sermon, but this new life remained basically reproductive. The goal was the Christian instruction of the people. The content was always derived from the storehouse of the Fathers. It is the Frankish church, however, which from the standpoint of preaching occupies an honored and exceptional position in the Middle Ages. Charlemagne clearly understood the church's task of nurturing the people, a responsibility which could not be discharged unless the sermon retained its status in the life of the cult. That position it had already begun to lose in many places. The laws of the land emphasized the duty of the priest to preach at the masses every Sunday and holy day. The Carolingian bishops strove to actualize their lords' intentions. In the year 797, Bishop Theodulf of Orléans exhorted his preachers: "He who knows the Scripture must proclaim the Scripture, but he who does not know it must at least impart the most well-known parts to the people, in order that they may escape the evil and do that which is good, seek peace and pursue it." The Latin verb *praedicare* now became the usual term for the task of the preacher. The objective was to translate the Gospel, every time it was read, into the language of the people and to explain it with the addition of useful exhortations. The interpretation could be based on the Epistle if this seemed more appropriate. We must recognize that there were differing ways by which the responsibility of preaching could be discharged, varying from a very simple interpretation of the content of the lections to a genuine homily which as a rule was taken from some collection of patristic sermons. The homilies of both Augustine and Caesarius of Arles were used in this manner. The Carolingian homiletical reform was able to attach itself to the living tradition of the church in Gaul largely because of Caesarius' influence. Moreover, emphasis on the baptismal confession and other simple basic texts was given a place alongside the exegesis of the lections. We find some evidence that the practice of adding a didactic and pastoral presentation to the exegesis of the text harks back to the Frankish church. All preaching in the church must serve to enlighten the people—thus the pedagogical motif again assumed a dominant position.

In the large Frankish bishoprics the sermon of necessity became the concern of the priests if it was to reach the people. This, however, was merely a postponement of the pedagogical problem since the question then became the education of the clergy. Here the church of the Frankish kingdom utilized the scholarly tradition from Britain and Italy. The preachers needed guidance and sermons which could be used as models. As a result, there arose a new homiletical literature, with very little originality, but characterized by a new concern for the inheritance from Christian antiquity. Two collections of homilies are the greatest monuments to the homiletical labors of the Carolingian Renaissance. The Lombard, Paul the Deacon, at Charlemagne's request wrote a collection of homilies intended for use by the clerics as readings for the canonical offices. This also contributed to a liturgical use of homiletical materials, a custom which has been continued in the short homily lections in the Roman breviary. Alcuin's compilation of homilies was designed to give the preachers source material for their exposition of the liturgical texts on Sundays. The collection was forgotten during the Middle Ages and was superseded by other compilations, the most important of which is the collection of homilies from the latter part of the ninth century by the abbot, later the archbishop, Rabanus Maurus, the most diligent biblical expositor in the later Middle Ages. Another contribution is again inseparably connected with the name of Alcuin, a contribution closely related to his collection of homilies. Through his influence the appointed pericopes gained the stability in the Western church which they have generally retained since that time. Charlemagne gave him the task of making a revision of the lectionary called *comes,* "companion." Of his own works, only the series on the Epistles is extant, but it is possible to reconstruct the general outline from other sources. This was not an original piece of work. What really happened was that the tradition which had developed in Rome and which was most probably later fixed by Gregory the Great was substituted for the old Frankish lectionary. The Frankish church thus made its own contribution to cultic life by aiding, through its adherence to the Roman tradition, in the development of a uniform order in the Latin West. This development would not have occurred except for the previous influences from the old Gallic church. We possess classic examples of this old Roman style of prayer in our collects. The order of pericopes which Luther inherited from the Middle Ages gained its essential pattern in Alcuin's revision. This is, perhaps, the most enduring contribution of the Frankish church to the history of preaching.

Preaching was diligently practiced in the centuries following the dissolution of the Frankish church, but the monuments preserved from this era exhibit little or no independence. The best may be characterized as sequels to the Carolingian Renaissance, which in its own era had lived on the inheritance from the ancient church. The chronicle preserves the name of many preachers, among them Ulrich of Augsburg in the tenth century, who had the ability to bring forth tears in his hearers, a gift highly prized in the Middle Ages. Anno of Cologne, in the eleventh century, could soften hearts of stone through his testimony to God's grace and righteousness. There are plentiful testimonies to the fact that preaching was regarded as the most important responsibility of the cleric. The era of missions still continued, the boundary between missionary areas and Christian lands being in a state of flux; for a long time, the newly Christianized masses needed elementary instruction and preachers had to combat widespread superstitious customs. The brief homilies which have been preserved from England, France, and Germany in the folk languages are the most interesting sermons from the standpoint of the history of culture. Their interest is largely limited to the manner in which Latin originals were re-worked; preaching had become an art in the use of borrowed materials. Natural gifts of oratory did make some original contribution, even in this era. It was difficult, however, for any medieval preacher to transcend the narrow boundaries of medieval thought.

The sermon had degenerated to a mechanical level and retained this status during the whole of the Middle Ages, even though it later developed into a rather unique artistic device. Some of the aids which were designed to make the work of the mechanic easier or to give him useful patterns for the embellishment of his work have their origin in this era. In Honorius' *Speculum Ecclesiae,* the preacher found both allegorical material for biblical exegesis and scholarly quotations from the literature of antiquity in an easily accessible form. During this period, *Master Physiologus,* a collection of animal legends, was compiled by an unknown author. In these legends, which derive from a Grecian source, the preaching cleric found a great number of bizarre stories and illustrations which, before they had been worn out by constant usage, must surely have awakened many a country community's living interest. Included in this collection was the history of the bird Phoenix, who set himself afire in order that later he might rise out of the ashes, and the story of the panther which represented the merciful Christ—he was beautiful and gracious, and his garments were mottled by more than twenty colors, representing the virtues of the Lord.

The Crusades and Bernard of Clairvaux

The renewal of preaching, which is one of the distinctive characteristics of the high Middle Ages, can be traced to three sources: the Crusades, the monasteries, and Scholasticism. These three factors are interwoven. The Crusades were significant because they gave oral proclamation a new and inspiring purpose. But all too soon the preaching of the Holy Cross was changed from a flaming personal testimony, as is the case with Saint Bernard, to a churchly routine, a mechanical task which to all intents and purposes developed alongside the practice of indulgences. It is a peculiar fact that preaching and indulgences stimulated each other. At first the preachers sought to awaken the desire to enter the Holy Land where people could win the complete forgiveness of their sins, but later they preached so as to make the indulgences granted by the Crusades desirable even after the hope of reconquering Palestine had long since died. They even preached on the special indulgence days set aside in different churches. The Crusade was soon directed against enemies other than the unfaithful on the other side of the ocean. A Crusade could be proclaimed against any enemy of the Holy Father, whether a rival for political power in Italy or the powerful heretical folk movements which, usurping a name taken from the storehouse of the Fathers, called themselves Manicheans. These movements, centered in Italy and Southern France, assumed the character of genuine folk religions and made use of traveling lay preachers: the intense struggle for their subjugation made its positive contribution by awakening popular preaching in the church to new life.

In Bernard (1090-1153) the enthusiasm of the Crusader and the asceticism of the monk joined hands. He stood in a dialectical relation to the contemporary development of Scholastic theology, as was expressed in his struggle with Abelard. In Bernard, brilliant gifts eventually broke through the mediocre pattern of plagiarism in order to make a creative contribution to preaching. Bernard won great reputation as a speaker preaching the Cross and working to convert the heretics in Languedoc. Known testimonies bear witness to the impression his fiery eloquence made upon those who did not even understand his language. The deepest secret of his power over the minds of men as a speaker, monastic leader, and churchman certainly lay in the fact that he was immediately grasped by the divine reality. In all ages this has continued to be the source of power for men of God. To this, however, we must add his purely human talents and his mastery of the art of persuasive speaking. His contemporaries tell us of his power but there are no documents which have preserved this testimony for subsequent generations. We are acquainted with Bernard the preacher only through his sermons delivered in the monastery, and his sermons for the seasons of the church year, saints' days, and sundry occasions. To this may be added his famous exposition of the Song of Solomon, an exposition which is constructed from homilies.

With the possible exception of the Irish-Scotch itinerant missionaries, preaching was hardly the special responsibility of the monks. The Cistercians were not popular preachers, since the requirements of their stable domicile hindered such a ministry. Not even within the monastery was preaching fostered. "As we off and on," it is stated in one of Bernard's sermons, "speak to you, contrary to the nature of our order, we do it not by our own presumptuousness, but at the behest of the venerable brothers and our fellow abbots, who give us such responsibilities as they will not give to themselves." The true preacher's unquenchable impulse to preach lived in Bernard paired with constant dread of the tremendous responsibility: "Why does the Lord," he said once, "ascend the mountain before he begins to teach, unless he wishes to teach us by this act that the preachers of God's word through the desire of their hearts and through their holy life must seek that which is above and ascend the mountain of virtue?" Bernard's extant sermons bear the marks of having been delivered to the monks not only at mass but whenever the common life in the order presented an opportunity. Monks from other orders were sometimes in attendance in the church or at the chapter auditorium in Clairvaux. The short monastery sermons, to which we must also add some memorial addresses for the dead, are exquisite productions of their kind. The form is often very simple but can, at times, rise to the level of an inspiring exultation which uses the whole register of the grand style of speaking. The medieval Latin assumes the color of the passionate love of Jesus. But at the same time that Bernard mediates the strangely fruitful motif of passion mysticism to the spiritual life of the Middle Ages and thus gives expression to solicitude for the world of the inner life, he is nevertheless dependent on the sermons of antiquity, above all on those of Augustine, for his preaching style. Thus, in the history of preaching, Bernard of Clairvaux is more specifically the last representative of patristic preaching than the initiator of a new epoch.

The Art of Preaching in Scholasticism

Older discussions of preaching during the Middle Ages have generally consisted of a series of descriptions of notable personalities who rose above the mass. Diligent research on preaching in the Middle Ages has lately been carried on with new zeal especially in France, England, and America which has given us a new picture. This research has confronted us with a great many sermon manuscripts which were previously unknown and which are yet to a degree uninvestigated. Special attention has been given both to the clarification of the highly developed preaching technique which is perhaps the primary contribution of the late Middle Ages in this area, and to an inventory of the surprisingly large number of technical books on the craft of the preacher. The work, which, to be sure, is often a routine and scarcely inspiring task, has drawn more attention to itself than it has to the great personalities.

The new influences which shaped the typical sermon in the late Middle Ages were also derived from monasticism, but in conjunction with the Scholastic theology of the universities. The logic of Aristotle became a factor in preaching and fostered a new awareness of the need for coherence and clarity. The union of Scholasticism and monasticism was actualized by the mendicant orders. This was a deviation from Francis' intentions but lay within the realm of Dominic's program for the preaching friars: the very name *fratres praedicatores* is a proof of the central place of preaching in the life of the church in the Middle Ages.

Preaching was carried on in the universities even before leadership in the theological task was transferred to the preaching friars and Minorites. From the very beginning the universities were clerical institutions, and sermons were both a part of the scholars' exercises and the responsibilities of the schoolmaster. The scholarly Latin sermon *ad clerum* was developed at the great seats of learning, Paris, Oxford, and others, so that it became an authentic artistic creation; it could by no means be immediately plagiarized by the parish priest or the mendicant friars for use as a popular sermon. Most certainly it was practical necessity which placed increased emphasis on the theory of preaching. This interaction between theory and practice was especially promoted by the mendicant orders, for the original popular orientation of the Minorities did not disappear even after their order had reached the heights of Scholastic scholarship in Bonaventure and Duns Scotus. Furthermore, the Dominicans, together with Bernard, were from the very first given the responsibility of converting heretics by better and more orthodox preaching. This was the background for their preoccupation with the technique of preaching.

The literature created by the work of the mendicant friars—the Dominicans, the Franciscans, and the Augustinian Anchorites—is of tremendous extent. Even a cursory knowledge of this production makes it evident that in this era the task of preaching was given serious consideration. Seldom, if ever, has the church exhibited a more serious concern. Within the mass of homiletical manuscripts, not considering collections of completed preaching series, we can distinguish three basic categories: handbooks on the art of preaching, collections of illustrations, and outlines.

We have knowledge of a great number of works on the art of preaching, *artes praedicandi*. T. M. Charland, a contemporary Dominican from French Canada, who has given exhaustive study to the matter,[1] has listed no fewer than one hundred fifty guides of this sort. Some of these are rather unimportant compilations, but many are complete dissertations which have been preserved in a number of manuscripts. The more thorough presentations are generally sermons addressed to the clergy and are primarily university sermons. We have already noted that we must regard popular preaching during the Middle Ages as an adaptation of scholarly preaching. Typical of the times is the fact that the two basic techniques received their names from the two leading centers of learning, Paris and Oxford. These two techniques, however, differ only in technical detail. The Paris technique was the less elaborate one.

In Charland's work, two English presentations, both from the fourteenth century, are readily accessible to us. The one, *Forma Praedicandi* ("The Form of Preaching") by Robert of Basevorn, fills ninety folio pages, and the other, *De Modo Componendi Sermones* ("The Method of Preparing Sermons") by the preach-

---

[1] *Artes Praedicandi, Contribution à l'histoire de la rhétorique au moyen âge* ("Publications de l'institut d'etudes médiévales d'Ottawa," Vol. I [1936]).

ing friar, Thomas of Waleys, is a bit shorter. Both are systematically arranged and both are mainly technical documents. Robert introduces his work with a definition of preaching and a statement as to who may lawfully preach. Thomas begins by exalting the office of the preacher, an office "more angelic than human." Thomas also gives the preacher good advice and helpful hints. He should certainly be careful not to preach if he is afflicted with a mortal sin, because then the sermon itself may also be a mortal sin. He must keep his task clearly in mind and seek the fountain of all wisdom in devout prayer. He must also, however, consider the externals, his attire, gestures, and above all his delivery. Before he appears publicly the inexperienced preacher should "first go to a place which is protected from the eyes of men, where he need not worry that any one can laugh at him and there he may begin to preach to the trees and stones and thus begin to train himself." He must be careful about his enunciation, not least the consonants *r* and *s*. The preacher must also be careful lest he tire his hearers and he must take his audience into account. He should not attack preachers' faults in a congregation of laymen nor attack the faults of laymen when he preaches *ad clerum*.

Our primary interest in these works is their proposed technique for the preparation of sermons. The preacher must first of all find a *thema* or subject. The sermon was often compared to a tree, such a tree being actually drawn in one of the homiletical manuscripts; the theme, naturally, was the trunk. The homileticians of the Middle Ages were well aware that the demand for a theme was a departure from the artless method of preaching practiced by the early church fathers, but they also understood that the inspiration of the Spirit had lifted the Fathers above the necessity of using the homiletical helps which their followers must employ. The whole sermon must grow organically from a theme taken from Holy Scripture, the theme for seasonal sermons at mass being taken usually from the Gospel or Epistle. To derive a theme from a nonbiblical liturgical text would have been a gross error. The sermon itself should be introduced by a prayer, the preacher admonishing his hearers to pray with him for the grace of the Holy Spirit. If the time was short, the preacher might proceed directly to the act of prayer with a few introductory words. The act of prayer then consisted in the common, perhaps silent reading of a well-known passage such as *Veni Sancte Spiritus, Ave Maria* or *Pater Noster.* Usually, however, the act of prayer was preceded by an introduction which began with a passage of Scripture either identical to the theme or related to it—a *prothema* or *antethema.* After the prayer, the theme was repeated, together with the citation of book, chapter, and verse. Sometimes a special introduction was added which should in some way illustrate or explain the theme by pointing an analogy or using an explanatory citation which did not need to be biblical. Here the risk of seeking to show off by means of irrelevant scholarly analysis was present. The homileticians suggested various methods for this introduction of the theme, *introductio thematis,* and warned against letting it be too expansive.[2] Next came the division or, as later expressed, the partition of the theme (*divisio thematis*) into two, three, or four parts, the threefold division being especially recommended as least apt to tire the hearer. It was also possible to divide the parts and even the subdivisions, but the preacher should not divide further. This great amount of division was of special help to him who otherwise had too little to say. The formulation of the rubrics of division required a great deal of attentive care and rhyming structures were often used. These instructions for division are very detailed and sometimes very finely drawn. Three words could be taken from the theme and the introduction could then be constructed from them, thus creating a

[2] *Introductio thematis,* the introduction of the theme, corresponds from a purely historical point of view to ancient rhetoric's requirement *captatio benevolentiae,* the device for capturing an audience's good will, or at least it serves the same purpose.

divisio intra; an external category could be appropriated and used to break the subject into usable parts, thus creating a *divisio extra.* Following the *divisio* a *declaratio et confirmatio partium* could follow, designed primarily to justify the partitioning and to show that it was in agreement with the Bible. Here a university preacher could also show off his exegetical learning.

All these items were the branches in the tree. Now, at last, came the completion of the divisions, a process by which the sermon took form. Here the preacher must correctly use and correctly group the material, which consisted of proof texts from the Bible and writings of the Fathers, with explanatory illustrations. A rich storehouse of these was available for use. In addition to these essential parts there were also a great many other artful ornaments which could make the whole even more artistic. To this must be added appropriate gestures, *gestus convenientia,* and becoming humor, *opportuna jocatio.*

The homileticians were by no means blind to the fact that concern for the form of the sermon could draw attention away from the content. Not least at the universities were those found who had high tastes and who could appreciate elegant *divisio* or an ingenious and scholarly *confirmatio.* Through recent investigations we have gained a good grasp of the academic preaching technique as it appeared in the great handbooks, but we lack knowledge how it was modified and applied. It is remarkable that the moralizing paranesis, the demand to follow the good and to flee the evil which assumed such a dominant place in the popular preaching, is hardly noticeable in the scholarly handbooks. We know of many conclusive instances which indicate that the age tired of artistry and longed for the simple biblical homily which the earlier Middle Ages had inherited from the ancient church. Wycliffe, especially, raised a protest against technical artificiality and demanded a simpler presentation of God's law and the word of salvation.

Simple biblical exposition certainly never ceased to exist in popular preaching and the tremendously extensive sources also exhibit a great deal of variation. We dare draw the tentative conclusion that the usual sermon walked a middle way. It continued to be expository by eliciting several main thoughts from the text and developing them with the help of the scholarly arsenal of homiletics, primarily by suitable illustrative stories and moralizing applications. This type of preaching is found in the Swedish postils which we possess from the Middle Ages. Despite its onesidedness, the demand for a specific subject and a logical introduction remain as the most important contribution of the Middle Ages to the development of preaching. Scholasticism and the mendicant orders created the method of preaching by a theme and developed outline, *modus . . . praedicandi per divisiones et per thema,* a method not unknown among us.

Homiletical Helps

Most recent investigations have made it clear that the sermon was an important factor in the development of popular literature during the Middle Ages.[3] The preacher's fondness for the illustrative anecdote brought forth a great many collections of examples, miracles, and similar anecdotes. This was the result of a slow development which is now very extensive and difficult to survey, a development which spread to all lands and left its traces in the literature of many nations. A large part of this material, loaned from one collection to the other and certainly minted in countless sermons, was borrowed from both heathen and Christian antiquities. A large number of fables and travel sagas were of Oriental origin.

Collections of sermonic illustrations were not peculiar to Scholasticism alone; they appear throughout the whole history of

[3] Cf. G. R. Owst, *Literature and Pulpit in Medieval England* (2nd rev. ed.; Oxford: B. Blackwell, 1961).

the Middle Ages. A certain collection of the lives of the Fathers which traced its origin to a late period in the ancient church retained its popularity for hundreds of years. The spiritual adventures of the sainted Egyptian monks became a treasured food for the soul even in Northern countries. *Gesta Romanorum* ("The Achievements of Rome") was another collection of illustrations from an earlier time. Gregory the Great's *Dialog Concerning the Lives and Miracles of the Italian Fathers* presented similar material. This collection was imitated in Caesarius of Heisterbach's *Dialogues Concerning the Miracles*. *Master Physiologus* provided a varied supply of animal fables. The rise of later specialized collections like the *Bee Book* by Thomas of Brabant, in which the life of the bee furnishes edifying anecdotes, proves that these types of illustration were highly regarded. There was also an *Ant Book* of similar type. The use of fables or other allegorical narratives gave rise to the so-called emblematic sermon, the purely parabolic sermon, which appears from time to time also in a later era. The *Legenda Aurea* ("Golden Legend") by Jacob of Voragine became the most-used collection of narratives concerning the saints. There were countless reworkings and assorted collections to lighten the task of the preacher. It is hardly necessary to recount the names: *Promptuarium Exemplorum* ("Prepared Illustrations"), *Hortulus Reginae* ("The Queen's Little Garden"), *Flores Virtutum* ("The Flowering of Virtue"), *Flores Doctorum* ("The Flowering of Learning"), etc.

The number of works shows that there was a lively demand for this type of literature. It is often impossible to establish the boundary between the sacred and the profane. It is the task of the literary historian rather than the historian of preaching to follow the development of the anecdote. There is, for example, a relationship between the illustrations used by preachers and the Italian Renaissance novel. Gabriel Barletta, the Italian Dominican, is in this respect the mediator. He won his fame through liberal use of the fascinating and often humorous anecdote.

Swedish literature in the Middle Ages is full of material from these collections of illustrations. Here we also find a *Lives of the Fathers*. In addition we have a whole shower of preaching fables in *Dyalogus Creaturarum Moralizatus* ("Dialogues of Moral Creatures"), one of the first books printed in Sweden; it furnished subjects for the artists who were busily covering the walls of the churches with moral pictures during the fifteenth century. The influence of medieval sermon illustrations may be traced in various directions. Many have not ceased being used even though their form has been altered. It would be interesting to investigate the degree to which specific motifs have survived. We should perhaps, at this point, especially keep in mind certain collections of allegorical illustrations which were especially popular, for example, *Castellum diaboli* ("The Devil's Citadel"), *Castellum Religionis* ("The Citadel of Religion"), or the "moralizing chess game" (*Moralitas de scaccario*) in which both the men and the moves were given symbolic meaning. It has been demonstrated that a similar motif was used in the Puritan sermon in England.[4] This is almost the same methodology that found its classic expression in *Pilgrim's Progress*.

Collections of illustrations were by no means the only homiletical helps of this kind. Collections of sentences and stories, both from the Bible and other books, have also been found. Journals on subject arrangement also existed. Not least do we find a whole array of collections of sermons and outlines, *parati sermones* ("prepared sermons"), and similar items. The most famous of these collections bears the ominous title *Dormi Secure*—"Sleep Securely." Its origin is a moot question but it was printed in many editions.

The most monumental example of the industry expended in

[4] C. Smyth, *The Art of Preaching* (London: SPCK, 1953), pp. 89 ff.

order to make the unsophisticated preacher's task easier is the large preaching lexicon. Several such books were printed. *Copia Exemplorum* ("The Copy of Illustrations") by Magister Mathias, Canon of Linköping, belongs in this category. The book testifies that the church of the late Middle Ages was anxious, even in Sweden, to furnish material for popular proclamation. *Summa Praedicantium,* which was compiled by the English Dominican John of Bromyard at the close of the fourteenth century, became the most famous and most-used lexicon. There was time for it to be printed twice before the Reformation, and at least two copies have been preserved in Swedish libraries. One of these, printed in Nuremberg in 1485, came from Vadstena. One can imagine the enchantment of the Brothers of Saint Birgitta with the tremendous folio—in modern printing it would easily fill three thousand pages. A long time would elapse before a homiletical work of similar inclusiveness could be produced. It is literally a lexicon, where we may turn to one hundred eighty-nine main words and find rich material to aid us whether we wish to preach on virtues or vices, about heaven or hell. Under each word we find subjects and divisions, with ample illustrative material. Here all sorts of collections of illustrations are melted together. A work of this type gives valuable insights into the thought world of the Middle Ages and presents us with living pictures from its life. It testifies to the importance attached to the craft of the preacher.

The Place of Preaching in the Late Medieval Church

To what extent and under what circumstances was all of this material on the craft of preaching practiced? The answer can only be given after we have thoroughly investigated the actual place of preaching in the life of the late medieval church. Certain basic outlines are clear.

The basic question is the true place of preaching. At the same time that the Carolingian Renaissance, by means of a series of directives emphasized the duty of explaining the gospel and of presenting certain simple truths, the general law of the church was concerned to limit the right to preach. The Carthusian and Albigensian traveling preachers, and the Lollards and Hussites toward the end of the Middle Ages, provided the occasion for the eagerness of the papacy to limit unauthorized and misleading preaching. A law from a council in the thirteenth century stated that unlearned and inexperienced priests must be careful when they preached to the people. Beyond this, in the late Middle Ages it was customary to give the right to preach to clerics who exercised the care of souls and to those who had been given such a dispensation by the pope. The mendicant friars especially, together with the Dominicans, Franciscans, and Augustinian hermits were included in the latter category. There was only one instance where a person who was not ordained to the priesthood or as a deacon could proclaim the word: an abbess, while not allowed to preach at mass, could deliver edifying addresses within the convent.

The mendicant orders pursued their calling as preachers with a great deal of care. Their scholarly training, which was especially required of the Dominicans, was primarily designed to prepare them for the task of preaching. As we have already emphasized, it was within these orders that the "new" preaching method developed. The privilege of hearing confessions was united with the responsibility of preaching and this became the occasion for conflict with the parochial priesthood who otherwise would gladly have left the drudgery of preaching to the traveling brothers. During the last centuries of the Middle Ages the secular priesthood became more and more negligent and the prelates, especially the bishops, set a very poor example for the preacher.

It is impossible to say to what extent sermons were delivered at the Sunday services in the parish churches. In his handbook designed for preachers, the scholarly Dean of Uppsala, Lawrence of Vaxala, gives a directive that the priest should present an exposition of the Gospel immediately following the Creed in the mass. Instead of being a regularly recurring element of the mass, the sermon increasingly was reserved for special days of penance and seasons of fasting, especially the Lenten season, when spiritual oratory flowed in rich measure, at least in the cities. To these we may add the great festivals and above everything else we must include the special days of indulgence. We have already noted that there was an intimate relationship between preaching and the practice of indulgences. This was not, however, the only situation where economic considerations played a part. The mendicant friars traveled to gather contributions for their monasteries and there were other more and less legitimate occasions for appealing to the generosity of the congregations. At some of the festivals the preachers could preach a very long sermon, but in the Middle Ages they usually observed a praiseworthy brevity and sought to retain living contact with their hearers. We do have a few very picturesque descriptions of the medieval listeners' reaction to their speakers.[5]

There were many occasions when sermons were considered as belonging to the order of the day—this was true of a bishop's visitation and similar festivals—and the handbooks from the Middle Ages list a whole catalog of such occasions. The rapidly increasing emphasis on the sermon left its mark on the large churches built by the mendicant orders. The pulpit became a usual fixture even though the very early pulpits were usually movable. Pews began to be customary. The friars, however, preached in many other places besides the sanctuary. Preaching to large crowds was conducive to open-air preaching even as during later periods of revival. Special preaching crosses, often

---

[5] See Owst, *Preaching in Medieval England* (Cambridge: Cambridge Univ. Press, 1926), pp. 169 ff.

magnificently ornamented, which perhaps called back memories of preaching during the Crusades, were raised in the church-yards and in public places. A story relates how Berthold of Ratisbon (Regensburg), the great and popular Franciscan preacher in thirteenth-century Germany, found the direction of the wind with a feather and then let the people settle down on the leeward side while he spoke from an improvised pulpit.

To describe the outer circumstances of preaching in the late Middle Ages is very difficult. We may say that its importance increased rather than diminished. The varying tendencies of the times, the Crusades, mysticism, the sometimes sickly and strained spirit of penance, paired with zealous meditation on the passion of Christ; all of these contributed toward making the need for diligent preaching greater. The mendicant orders' traveling preachers bit by bit lost their influence, even though the Italian Franciscan John of Capistran did make a tremendous impression by his Crusade sermons as late as the fifteenth century. Indulgences and Crusades were closely related. Listening to sermons was itself a good work and could be rewarded by indulgence privileges. John Eck in Ingolstadt, a surprisingly diligent preacher, made it clear that he who devoutly listens to a sermon performs a work which is just as meritorious as the work of the Carthusian who scourges himself. The plenary indulgence, typical of the expiring Middle Ages, made the oral proclamation its servant. This proclamation very often assumed the character of violent penance preaching, but as soon as the indulgence itself became the goal rather than a pedagogical method, it was a sign of the church's decadence. These signs increase in the centuries prior to the Reformation.

On the other hand, a real concern for preaching appears in the special preaching missions which were instituted in many cities, especially in Germany. The best-known example is the *praedicatur* which was instituted for Geiler of Kaisersberg in Strasbourg's cathedral church in the year 1479. It was his duty to preach every Sunday, daily during Lent, and also on special holidays and procession days. The tremendous literature on preaching continued to expand. Such men as Nicholas of Cusa, Gabriel Biel, and many others made their contribution to it. We do, however, search in vain for a new living fountain to water the dry ground of the mechanical address. Originality in style and choice of subject was by no means lacking—at times it bordered on the burlesque, but the storehouse of thought remained hardly new or creative. At the same time we cannot deny that preaching in the late Middle Ages exhibited tremendous inclusiveness. National characteristics appear much more powerfully than in earlier periods and make their contribution. The old-fashioned parish sermon in the mass dies out and with it, perhaps, also the artless pattern of the homily. On the other hand, however, the masses gather around famous orators in the cities and Lent is celebrated with an edifying torrent of words which has hardly been surpassed in the church of the Reformation.

Use of the Bible

One task remains. With the help of the three basic elements of the sermon we must make an attempt to bring order out of these varied and contradictory impressions.

Did the Middle Ages really value and proclaim a biblical message? It is not possible to give a simple answer. An inventory of the extensive sources would show that the age by no means lacked diligent scriptural expositors. We scarcely discover any counterparts to the comprehensive patristic expositions of complete books of the Bible. In this area also the greatest contributions came from mendicant friars such as Cardinal Hugh of St. Cher (d. 1267) who handed down a tremendous postil, and Nicholas of Lyra, a Grey Friar (d. 1346) who was the greatest or at least the most imaginative exegete of the Middle Ages.

A number of textual expositions are very naturally included among the many available practical homiletical aids. The impact in this realm of works from the preceding centuries appears in the plenaries of the late Middle Ages which contain the texts for all the days of the church year and often include expositions. It was, however, the pericope system that made the continuous exposition of the Bible less desirable. Full justice to exegetical preaching was done when the old sample method of preaching, borrowed from the ancient church, directly exegeted the Epistle and Gospel for the day. The exponents of the Scholastic method were also interested in anchoring their preaching in Scripture. The demand was unalterable that the sermon must relate itself to a biblical text. During this period, this meant that the theme must be derived from the Bible. This also implied that the development of the parts of the sermon must be supported by a clear word of Scripture.

A sense of tragedy, however, rests upon the attempt of the Middle Ages to be faithful to the Bible. The very urge to use the Bible contributed toward making it a sealed book. The preachers of the Middle Ages had assumed heavy liabilities by making the inheritance from the ancient church their own, as they, within the context of the Latin tradition, acknowledged and further developed the legacy from Origen. Not only double but triple meanings, the *literal,* the *moral* or *tropological,* and the *allegorical,* were included in their technique of exegesis. Sometimes a fourth, the *anagogical,* was added. Jerusalem, for example, which signified the capital of Judea in the literal sense, meant morally or tropologically an orderly state and community life, allegorically the church, and anagogically the holy city, eternal life. It was very natural to the mood of the Middle Ages to see a hidden meaning behind every clear word. In this manner the possibility for real exegetical preaching was destroyed by the method of exegesis itself. Even the preachers who like Berthold of Ratisbon attempted to base their sermons on Scripture were content to select suitable proof texts without giving thought to their essential content and context. The unity of the Bible was destroyed by isolated oracular statements. The basic rule of interpretation became the fact that everything must mean something besides the explicit.

This misuse of Scripture was, perhaps, most highly developed by the "most spiritual" preachers of the Middle Ages, notably by Eckhart. A Platonic orientation created an inner rapport between him and Origen. This can also be affirmed of Tauler, since the biblical pericopes which he treats are given significance only as symbols of an event in the life of the soul. Practical exegesis was used more simply in popular preaching—most often to draw out from the text some usable peg on which the preacher could hang his message. Extant Swedish collections of homilies give some examples of this, as when the feeding of the five thousand is exegeted, the seven loaves become the virtues which Christ gives his servants. We should be able to make a rather interesting excursion into the labyrinth in which Middle Ages biblical research was enclosed. The result would, however, not be worth the effort. The scholars and preachers searched in vain for a way out of these erroneous paths, but they did not find it where they had hoped it might appear. Even the great preachers, such as Berthold or Savonarola, merely used a specific passage of Scripture as a crutch or projectile and stopped at this point.

We expect great things of Wycliffe and his school; the study of his extant sermons has, however, disappointed those who wish to see in him a "precursor" of the Reformation. Though his Latin sermons are wholly Scholastic in character, the English sermons are a practical, popular proclamation based upon the Bible. The allegorical method, does, however, hold him in its sway and when he interprets Scripture literally it becomes primarily a law of God which demands application to the contemporary situation in church and state. Because of this Wycliffe did not find the true living water of the gospel. It was in rapture over the law of God that the Lollards left on their travels. The preaching of the law of God was given an even sharper edge by being transferred to Bohemian soil and blended with Czech nationalism, but it certainly did not gain any depth or originality. It was the humanistic biblical theology which first opened the way to wider and more free horizons. For a long time, however, this theology carried with it some of the dead weight of Platonism from the Florentine Academy and therefore, especially in Erasmus himself, it exhibited a moralizing character which obscured basic evangelical motifs. Yet, even during the late Middle Ages, traces are found of a more artless exegesis of the pericopes. The parish priest must explain his text *plane et intelligibiter,* as plainly and intelligently as he could.

From the Middle Ages the Roman church took over an exegetical tradition which, in spite of the negative reaction to Wycliffe, was determined by the same view of Scripture which Wycliffe espoused. According to the Tridentine Profession it was the duty of the preacher, *sacram scripturam divinamque legem annuntiare,* to proclaim the Holy Scripture and the law of God.

Liturgical and Prophetic Elements

The basic pattern of the sermon during the Middle Ages was liturgical. Within the solemn context of the mass the priest was to exegete the pericope for the day. This was one of the most significant contributions of the Middle Ages to the development of preaching, even though it stands in a certain inner tension with another major medieval contribution, the Scholastic method. Very often, however, the propers for saints' days most likely interested the preachers and the hearers more than the propers for the seasons. The extent to which the normal pericope sermon was preserved in the mass is a debatable question; it does seem certain that such preaching did occur less often. The placement of the sermon in this traditional context was, however, not without significance for the very structure of the act of preaching itself. The Scholastic sermon also presupposed the mass as its natural framework and it sought its subject in one of the prescribed biblical texts.

The fact that the sermon creates a liturgical shell around itself is part of its uniqueness. During the Middle Ages this occurred in the development of a peculiar form of devotion which was given the name *offene Schuld*,[6] a confession of sin and absolution —and perhaps other liturgical elements as well—added to the sermon. The form most likely originated in the Carolingian era but formulas for the practice do occur in the homiletical journals of the high Middle Ages and they can be noted in handbooks as late as the dawning sixteenth century. Besides the act of confession itself, which was significant as a preparation for the celebration of the sacrifice of the mass rather than for the communion, the rite also included the catechetical passages which the church of the Middle Ages continued to impress on the minds of the people: the Creed and the Lord's Prayer, perhaps a Hail Mary, an intercession for the living and the dead and various messages concerning saints' days, times of fasting and other subjects. In this practice, the spread of which cannot be exactly determined, the Middle Ages bequeathed a component of worship and preaching which would gain homiletical and liturgical significance in later times.

---

[6] [In the English rite, the vernacular devotions, instructions, and notifications which were attached to the sermon were known as the "prone." The prayers for the several classes of the living and the lately departed were called the "bidding of the bedes." See Brightman, *The English Rite* (London: Rivingtons, 1915), II, 1020-1045. Luther D. Reed, *The Lutheran Liturgy* (Rev. ed.; Philadelphia: Muhlenberg Press, 1947), pp. 316 ff. discusses the relation of the prone to the prayer of the church in the liturgy.—TRANSLATOR.]

In general, however, it is true that the liturgical context of the mass constricted and impoverished the sermon and in return contributed very few life-giving impulses to it. The sermon which blossomed most richly during the last centuries of the Middle Ages to a great degree freed itself from its envelopment in the mass. The traveling mendicant friars often delivered their sermons outside of the context of the liturgical service. The sermon which gained great popularity and became a significant influence in the lives of the people in the late Middle Ages was a special rather than regular form of preaching. This influence on the crowds depended to some degree on the fact that such preaching was concentrated in the periods of fasting. Situations when a sermon could be presented were manifold, but among these the parish sermon in the regular Sunday mass began to fade into the background.

The prophetic element in medieval preaching encompassed, on the one hand, every orientation to the present, every direct address to the immediate situation, and, on the other hand, markedly personal contributions. It is difficult to establish exact boundaries for such preaching as over and against clearly pedagogical proclamation. Pedagogical preaching belongs to periods when foundations are laid and this was especially the case in the Carolingian kingdom and in other sections of the Germanic churches. The emphasis on popular nurture diminished during the course of the centuries but it was never completely absent. We can, furthermore, ask whether or not preaching during the Middle Ages also included a purely pastoral orientation, but the question cannot be easily answered. The care of souls belonged in the context of penance rather than preaching. Some general guidance for the soul did, however, often appear in sermonic suggestions concerning that which one must seek and that which one must avoid. We should, perhaps, be able to find examples of a more thoroughgoing analysis of the state of the soul and its needs in German mysticism.

We cannot deny that the preachers of the Middle Ages had a broad practical orientation. We can rather accuse them of having had too great a tendency to moralize, to allow every text in the Bible to become the starting point for an ethical admonition which often was primarily intended to emphasize the church's precepts on penance, fasting, and good works. On the other hand, it would be unfair not to acknowledge the moral pathos which sometimes gave this moralism a measure of the authentic severity of the law. Criticism of the shortcomings of the clergy was often astonishingly severe and sometimes it almost became a recurrent item on the agenda at priestly gatherings, where it was usually presented in Latin. The popular attacks on the extravagance and offences of the prelates, which appeared during the late Middle Ages and the time of the Reformation, were to a great degree anticipated in these addresses to the clergy or in the collections from which they gleaned their material.

The open-hearted critique of unsatisfactory conditions in the secular community, which appears in many places in the church's preaching, is more interesting. Socially oriented sermons were by no means lacking in the Middle Ages. This was especially true in England where a plentiful supply of sources has been the occasion for interesting research.[7] This is apparent in the social ballads which appeared toward the end of the fourteenth century, the best-known example of which is *The Vision of Piers Plowman* (c. 1362). To a great degree this deals with material which had earlier been homiletically used. Bromyard's *Summa Praedicantium,* which summarized the results of the preaching of the mendicant orders during the thirteenth and fourteenth centuries, is a rich source for such criticism of social evils. The religious contributions in the social crisis of the late fourteenth century in England are on the whole very interesting because in

[7] See G. R. Owst, *Literature and Pulpit in Medieval England* (1st ed., 1933), especially the chapter "The Preaching of Satire and Complaint."

this context preaching was truly a factor in the life of the times. The social criticism was presented in radical form by Wycliffe's "poor priests." The same pattern may also be observed in Wycliffism's offshoot, the Hussite movement in Bohemia. Social satire found its most original representative on the continent in the person of Geiler of Kaisersberg.

The Influence of Personalities

The tendency of recent research in the history of preaching to show greater interest in technique than in personalities has to a degree been a sound reaction against the opposite over-emphasis. The description of an epoch would, nevertheless, be misleading if we were to ignore the mountaintops which rise above the surrounding lowlands. Every careful study of great personalities contains a dangerous tendency to open the perspective so that it destroys the context. After Saint Bernard, who is enthroned in isolated majesty as the last of the church fathers, high peaks are not frequent.

A chronicler has penned the words, "God made his mouth a sharp sword" concerning the German Grey Friar, Berthold of Ratisbon (d. 1272), who is named after the city where he died. He attained legendary fame. Enormous crowds gathered in the open fields to hear him and miracles occurred at his grave. No other person gives us such a vivid impression of the strength of the medieval sermon at its zenith. He epitomized all of the typical elements in the homiletical tradition of the era. He drew freely upon the Fathers and Bernard and did not hesitate to use Augustine's crow which cried *cras, cras.* Often he preached on the pericopes, and therefore he certainly must have sometimes spoken from within the solemn context of the mass. He also made careful use of the Scholastic technique. He could make use of arresting illustrations or engage the interest of his hearers by means of a fictitious dialog. He could speak on the seven planets, and on the open book of nature where God had written his word just as he had in the Scripture. The Platonic trait of desire is not missing in his description of the loving Father's beauty. This whole highly diversified equipment is, however, carried and made alive by original individuality, a man who uses his playful fantasy and his popular gift of oratory to awaken love to God and man in human hearts, to warn against vice by sometimes using the completely gruesome apparatus of the sermon that smelled of brimstone, and to make virtue worthy of desire. (A great many of his sermons are extant in the form of transcriptions which have been collected in a book which bears the title *Rusticanus*. The book has a varied history of usage and its textual history is very complicated.) Berthold was the classical preacher of the Middle Ages and more than any other he embodied the living powers of his own times.

Most of the outstanding preachers in the late Middle Ages came from the Dominican order. Within this compass it is not possible for us to stop and consider Berthold's younger contemporary, Brother Peregrinus of Poland, who is especially interesting as an example of the vulgar oratory which could draw people to the preaching sites established by friars. Dominican preaching rises to other, sometimes dizzy heights in the German mystics. From Peter of Dacia we are acquainted with the spiritual hothouse atmosphere which appeared especially in the convents of the sisters, where those who were concerned with the care of souls were acquainted with the secrets of the inner life. The work of Meister Eckhart (d. c. 1328) must generally be viewed as arising out of this background. His extant sermons were delivered to the circle of the initiated, who were able to follow his speculations concerning God and the soul; concerning the Godhead as the highest being, *die ungenature Natur* who has implanted the spark of the divine in man *das Fünkelein;* concerning the Son's birth in the soul which in complete denial of the world, in total *Gelassenheit,* is able to accept the divine infusion. Some of Eckhart's writings are rather lectures, collations of addresses delivered at intimate gatherings in the monastery community. His message, presented in language which makes him a classic figure of German literature, is not basically original. The classical Bernardian emphasis on the love of Jesus runs through his thought as does also the Thomistic theology which he never consciously abandoned. Basically, Eckhart's theology was the upsurge of the mighty flood of Neo-Platonic mysticism, which does not observe the boundaries between religious denominations and confessions, and which appeals to mystically oriented men in every age by its strangely intimate tones.

John Tauler (d. 1361) certainly plants his feet more firmly in the stream of churchly preaching than his great teacher Eckhart. His long period of service in Strasbourg has contributed toward making this city a classical site in the history of Christian oratory. Even though the problems of authenticity are difficult to solve, we certainly do have a significant collection of his genuine sermons which were generally delivered on the pericopes of the missal. He does not wholly despise the rules for the methodical construction of the thematic sermon but they are used with a great deal of freedom. Sometimes the pattern becomes textually analytic, although the content is hardly determined by the word of Scripture; at other times pure formlessness seems to predominate. For Tauler, as well as for all mystics, all things external properly have meaning only for those who dwell in the forecourt. For the esoteric circle, the word of the Bible is also subservient to inner enlightenment. Tauler seems to proclaim the act of God in the atonement in accents which seem to be wholly evangelical; he seems to open the way to complete fellowship with God through simple faith which depends only on Christ's merit; but basically he lives in Eckhart's world of thought and faith where the divine can only be delineated by the method of negation. This is "the divine darkness," which because of its unspeakable brilliance is opaque to all human understanding. Here the goal is complete union with God, which is won by way of the mystical stages, and it leads to complete absorption where all distinctions cease.

It is not our task to seek to analyze the Christian content of mystical preaching, of which Tauler is the greatest representative. Instead we must consider his preaching as an example of a deep artery within Christendom which swells up from time to time and often causes the words of the preacher to be characterized by a glowing fire. We may be uncertain whether or not the preachers of a timeless mysticism should be numbered among the prophetic preachers who are known primarily for their address to the specific contemporary situation. There are, however, occasions when such a timeless sermon seems to be peculiarly appropriate. We may also question whether or not Eckhart's and Tauler's extant writings, in spite of their pattern as sermons, are genuinely homiletical, but it is generally not possible to draw a sharp distinction between the homily and the devotional treatise. This is especially evident if we continue tracing the development from Tauler to Henry Suso and to the Dutch mysticism which flowered at Deventer, Zwolle and Groenendael. The spoken word was certainly a power in this movement, which established its external pattern in the congregation at Windesheim in the Netherlands and in the Brethren of the Common Life. This piety found its classic expression in *The Imitation of Christ* and the sermons which Thomas à Kempis left behind. From these sources we gain a perspective on the intimate but somewhat narrow world of late medieval piety. Here we find a rich area of research for him who wishes carefully to investigate the boundary between preaching and proper devotional literature. Between preaching and devotion a living mutality has held sway in all ages.

On an *a priori* basis we would lean in the direction of classifying Wycliffe as a prophetic personality. We have previously noticed how he, in spite of his biblicism, hardly won through to the deeper understanding of Scripture which we would have expected. Neither do we meet in him the spontaneous spiritual power which creates a great preacher. Prophetic characteristics, however, were not absent. His preaching became in the highest degree an instrument of actual spiritual warfare. His pungent artlessness, which consciously differentiated itself from subtle technique and rhetorical embellishment, anticipates the Puritanism of a later era. Wycliffe, however, cannot claim the same place of honor in the history of homiletics as he does in the history of dogma and church politics.

Lastly there remain two personalities who require our attention. Geiler of Kaisersberg (d. 1510), one of the few preachers of the late Middle Ages who did not belong to a monastic order, became famous primarily by scourging the sins of the time in popular language. In many respects he reminds us of Berthold of Ratisbon but he is hardly to be numbered among the great spirits. Nevertheless, he is one of the most characteristic personalities in the preaching of the late Middle Ages; many lines of previous development converge in him, notably the Scholastic method, the rich use of illustrations, the more simple motif of mysticism, and the popular art of oratory as exemplified in the mendicant friars. He understood the art of captivating the masses as few have who came either before or after him, and some of his subjects have become classic. With great delight he employed the "emblematic" method which fully allegorized the prescribed frame of reference, as, for example, when he delivered seventeen sermons on the lion which was exhibited in the market place in Strasbourg. But the bizarre flashes of wit and the affable burlesque which sometimes appear were not ends in themselves. They were the means of reaching men with a highly relevant message of repentance which, nevertheless, failed to achieve its purpose since it did not arrive at a point where it could make the deepest ethical motivations in the gospel effective.

The preacher in the cathedral in Florence, Girolamo Savonarola (d. 1498) had much wider dimensions. Here it is not possible to describe the passionate drama which led the Dominican monk from Bologna to the position of spiritual dictator in the city of the Medicis and finally to the stake on Piazza della Signoria; nor is it possible to analyze the basic elements in the spiritual equipment of his fiery soul: Thomism, Franciscan love of Christ, the apocalypticism of Joachim of Fiore and a prophetic consciousness of vocation. The apparent degeneracy of the Renaissance in the merchant houses on the Arno as well as in the papal city provided a splendid background for his flaming message of repentance which centered on the proclamation of an imminent judgment on the decadent church. Hardly ever in the history of the church has the spoken word exhibited such power over the minds of men. The picture of Savonarola's preaching which his hearers have presented diverges sharply from his written legacy. In his writings it is still possible, to a greater extent than is generally the case with preachers of repentance, to recapture something of the original fire. In a sermon on the Seventy-third Psalm he describes the vision of a glorious temple being torn down—this is the destiny of the depraved church. A sermon on repentance from Matt. 4:17 delivered in the cathedral in Florence on November 1, 1494, gives us the opportunity of listening to his eager address to the various estates of depraved Florence. In this instance also, the power of the address was certainly due primarily to that peculiar magnetism which usually is the secret of personal influence. Savonarola left behind him a whole series of sermons on biblical books but his textual method did not rise above the usual atomism of the Middle Ages. We lack evidence as to whether or not his preaching rose out of the context of the mass; for him, however, the liturgical context was never very significant. Savonarola is thus the foremost preacher in the Middle Ages to show us how prophetic preaching breaks the shackles of inherited forms but in so doing also limits its own influence. A brilliant episode appears before us, but it is not organically related to the later development.

It has only been possible to consider a very limited number of basic types in the changing pattern of medieval preaching. No matter how often we immerse ourselves in its history, we are astonished by its breadth and by the zeal with which the task of preaching was carried on, but at the same time we must make the disheartening observation that the fruit of the labor was very meager. In part this was due to the fact that the basic elements of the sermon were not brought together in harmonious co-operation. In its attempt to become biblical, preaching lost its hold on the reality of the biblical revelation and thus stopped up its own fountain. The liturgical context became a straitjacket instead of a support. The most gifted men who were conscious of having a prophetic mission destroyed the forms which the sermon needed for fruitful work in the everyday world.

FIVE

From Luther to Carpzov

Luther's Preaching

Once, at table in Wittenberg, Luther related that Staupitz had given him the commission to preach "under this pear tree." The fifteen various reasons Luther claimed to have given as a defense were of no avail. This is said to have happened in connection with the granting of the degree of doctor of theology in the year 1512. Actually, however, Luther hardly could have escaped from the responsibility of preaching in Erfurt as early as 1509. The starting point of his preaching must remain uncertain; the extremity can be exactly dated: February 15, 1546, three days before his death. Between these points there coursed a preaching ministry which has few parallels in the history of the church. The extant sermons are estimated at about twenty-three hundred, many of them being found in various recensions. Luther's work is significant in the history of preaching as a new beginning even though we may be uncertain about its scope and content.

The fact that Luther's preaching has never become the object of a thoroughgoing examination is a noticeable loss. Older studies have all too often skimmed the surface, or they have been content with a panegyrical treatment. Newer researches have to some extent concerned themselves with involved textual historical problems or limited themselves to special tasks of measurable extent.[1] Research has hardly come further than a general survey of the contours of the sources.

[1] [The literature on Luther's preaching is remarkably scanty, and what does exist is very often not available in libraries. Primary sources for those who wish to read Luther's sermons in English include the fifty-

Following the best tradition of the mendicant orders, the Augustinian hermits were concerned about training good preachers. The commission to preach was first given by the Vicar General, usually a few years after ordination and subsequent to the time when the candidate had been given special training for the task. In Luther's case the commission to preach was closely related to his doctorate in the Holy Scriptures. During the first years he had addressed the brothers in the refectory, but in the year 1514 he received the additional commission to preach in the Wittenberg city church and he continued to do this regularly until Bugenhagen became chief pastor in 1522. In addition he continued preaching the word in the monastery and speaking at many special occasions in the castle church as well as on visits which he made on behalf of the order in various places. The first period in his ministry has been variously dated but under no circumstances can it be extended further than 1521. The sermons of his youth as well as the first examples of his purely reformatory preaching are thus included within this compass.

This first period is of the greatest interest for historical understanding. In Latin outlines and fragments from the years 1512 to 1515, we meet the monastery preacher trained in Scholastic technique. With the aid of material from the Scriptures, with the Aristotelian logical apparatus, and with the prolog of John's Gospel as text, we hear him develop the mystery of the

five-volume translation now in progress, *Luther's Works,* eds. Jaroslav Pelikan and Helmut T. Lehmann (Philadelphia and St. Louis: Fortress Press and Concordia Press, 1955-); an earlier six-volume edition, *Luther's Works* (Philadelphia: Muhlenberg, 1915-32); and the thirteen-volume edition edited by J. N. Lenker (Minneapolis, 1903-1910).

E. C. Kiessling, *The Early Sermons of Luther and Their Relation to the Pre-Reformation Sermon* (Grand Rapids, Mich.: Zondervan, 1935) is short but interesting. In the introduction to *Luther's Sermons I* ("Luther's Works," Vol. LI, 1959), pp. xi-xxi, from the series just cited, John W. Doberstein has a short monograph on Luther's preaching. Roland H. Bainton, *Luther's Meditations on the Gospels* (Philadelphia: Westminster Press, 1962), pp. 11-20, makes some observations on Luther's preaching.—TRANSLATOR.]

Trinity. But the claws of the lion are already evident! It was not unusual for Luther to write sermons for others. Thus, as early as 1512, he furnished the text of a synodical sermon in the monastery of the Premonstratensian Canons (Norbertines) in Leitzkau. Here a systematically constructed analysis is interrupted by a flaming admonition to the priests not to desert their most important task, the preaching of the word. But he also speaks of the presence of Christ in the heart through faith in a way that anticipates the mystical period in his preaching, a period which covers the years 1515 to 1517. In the extant sermons from these years we are met by gentle, wistful tones which exhibit the influence of Tauler and the *Theologia Germanica*. These stand in singular contrast to the sword thrusts and boisterous polemic of the Reformer's later style of preaching. In the year 1516 he preaches on a word in the Magnificat, of how the blessedness of the holy virgin consisted in her complete passivity. Nevertheless, new designs appear even before the mystic melody has had time wholly to disappear. A sermon preached in 1516, a year earlier than the posting of the Ninety-five Theses, attacks the practice of indulgences and is of interest also as an example of Luther's homiletical development. He derives a sentence out of the text on Zacchaeus which has some of the characteristics of a developed preaching theme, "To those for whom Christ is significant all other things are as nothing. But for those to whom Christ is of no significance all other things are always great." When on Sexagesima Sunday, 1517, he criticizes the conduct of preachers and monks, which is a witness to the unfruitful soil in their hearts, he has hardly passed the boundaries of medieval criticism of the church.

A few sermons in German from the year 1518 give us a picture of Luther's typical sermons before he had developed his own style. On the Ember days, Wednesday and Friday during Lent, he spoke on the various Gospel lessons. On the Wednesday after Laetare (the Fourth Sunday in Lent), he preached on the text concerning the man born blind as it is found in John, chapter 9. He used the text allegorically: he who does not understand the hidden secrets of God is blind. Traces of the mystical influence were still present, but the tone had become more popular and the criticism of the church had become sharper.

The basic series of catechetical sermons also belongs to these years of transition. Luther set about, in accordance with medieval practice, to add a pedagogical exposition of the Commandments and the Lord's Prayer to his Sunday sermon in the mass, which was based on a short *exordium*. Here the term *exordium* gains its own status; more exactly it corresponds to the *antethema* of the Middle Ages. Luther's *exordia* sermons were later printed from a manuscript which is not now extant. During the years 1515 to 1517 Luther used this method in preaching on the Decalogue and in this way, according to Oecolampadius, he drew "the veil from Moses' face." The published series of 1518, *Decem praecepta Wittenbergensi praedicata populo* ("Ten Sermons on the Ten Commandments Preached to the People in Wittenberg") is one of the basic sources for Luther's work on the catechism. Ten more years would elapse before he had completed this work. [The catechetical sermons of 1528 were the basis for The Large Catechism.] The Lord's Prayer was treated in a similar manner. It often happened that Luther's works were the product of an auditor who let his notes be published. Luther's *Auslegung deutsch des Vater unsers für die einfältigen Laien* ("German Exposition of the Lord's Prayer for Simple Folk") came later (1519). Here we meet the constant interaction between the pulpit and the printing press which is so characteristic of Luther's literary production. The evangelical sermon showed itself to be a very useful commodity which could profitably be exploited by the printer and the book salesman in a time when literary copyrights were unknown.

It is very obvious that in the Reformation sermon the catechetical motif quickly overshadowed the basic homiletical element. The

unique double form, a catechetical exposition added to the sermon on the Gospel, became common in the Lutheran territorial
churches. In addition to the catechetical series, Luther also delivered serial expository sermons on various sections of Scripture.
The weekly program in Wittenberg presented an opportunity
for a large number of spiritual addresses. Three sermons were
usual on Sunday: in the morning, a sermon at five or six o'clock
on the Epistle, and again at eight or nine (within the mass) on
the Gospel; in the afternoon serial treatment of some particular
book of the Bible. There was also preaching on every day of
the week: Monday and Tuesday on the catechism, the remaining
days on various books of the New Testament. It is difficult to
determine the exact extent of Luther's share in this tremendous
program. The primary responsibility for the services in the parish
church naturally fell to Bugenhagen after he had assumed the
post of chief pastor of the parish in 1522.

The reformatory character appears most sharply in the sermons
for special occasions, such as the sermon in the Leipzig castle
church in 1519 or the sermon on the road to Worms in 1521.
This is also true of the sermons on special subjects. Several of
the treatises from these years are doubtless to be considered as
re-worked sermons. In isolated instances, such as in *Sermo de
triplici justitia* ("Treatise on the Triple Righteousness") of 1518,
we are able to detect a homiletical orientation in the extant text,
but in most cases the sermon has become a literary form which
has lost the marks of the oral presentation.

The most noteworthy examples of occasional preaching are the
eight Invocavit sermons delivered in Wittenberg the week following the First Sunday in Lent, 1522. Their powerful influence
in promoting a more measured cultic reform in contrast to the
radical stream which had carried Carlstadt away is well known.
The extant manuscripts, which are based on the notes of hearers,
hardly retain the impression of the power of the spoken word.
These textless addresses formally exhibit the inclusiveness of

the concept of the sermon in an era when the *sermo* was an event rather than a product of the writing table.

The beginnings of the church postil antedate the Invocavit sermons. This medieval designation for a collection of expositions of the pericopes intended to be delivered *post illa verba* ("after these words," i.e., after the reading of the pericopes) became a generally used term in Lutheran families. The church postil became the classic monument to Luther the preacher and it exhibits both his greatness and his limitations. It is, however, only to a small degree an exhibit of his style of speaking, and its origin and textual history makes it a very complicated document. At the request of the elector Luther also prepared a collection of model sermons designed as helps for naive preachers. The advent section appeared in the year 1521. Along with the translation of the Bible Luther worked in the Wartburg on a continuation of the postils through the Epiphany season. This festival was treated in a small dissertation of more than 100 pages. This earliest complete section of the postils generally bears the marks of having been composed at the writing desk. Three years later Luther himself continued the collection to include Lent. It was, however, only the "winter postil" which had been edited by Luther himself. The summer section was produced as a compilation by Luther's admirers and the copyist Stephen Roth, and was published in the year 1526. This was an uncritical piece of work in which all available material was used and where fragments from other preachers were sometimes inserted alongside the genuine passages from Luther. The genuine passages were also treated very arbitrarily. A new summer postil, edited at the request of Luther by Kaspar Cruciger, appeared later (1544).[2] This postil, which was based on both Gospel and Epistle texts,

---

[2] [Brilioth mistakenly dated this publication 1549. All authoritative sources use the date 1544, two years prior to Luther's death in 1546.— TRANSLATOR.]

seems to be even more free than Roth's work, but it does contain sermons from Luther's later life and it does exhibit a spirit of congeniality with the life of the master.

The house postil's origin has also a similar history. The material consists mainly of sermons which Luther delivered in his home during times when he was hindered by sickness from appearing in church, especially during the years 1532 to 1534. From his own notes Veit Dietrich edited and published a very free revision in 1544, which gave the house postil its general outlines, even though there was in this connection also a later attempt to revise and correct the text.

Even though the postils became the basic sources for the transmission of Luther's preaching to later eras, we may say that these works are only a minor part of the rich homiletical material, which as yet has not been thoroughly investigated. Throughout his whole life the reformer continued to be a tireless speaker. On most holidays he preached twice; one Sunday in 1531 as often as four times. During the year 1529 it is reported that he spoke three or four times a week. The extant manuscripts make it possible for us at certain points to follow him day after day: we have such a continued series for Easter, 1529. The catechetical sermons of 1528 were later revised to become The Large Catechism of 1529. Luther was fond of dealing serially with biblical texts in the sermons which he delivered during the week and on Sunday afternoons; thus during 1523 he went through I Peter and in 1528 he covered Jesus' farewell discourses in John. He also treated several books of the Old Testament in a similar way. Luther's preaching prior to 1521 has been very carefully studied, but his homiletical production during the last two decades of his life has most often been treated in a cursory manner. Here a more careful inventory and analysis would be very welcome.

The Shape of the Sermon

Luther has not given us any summary presentation of his thoughts on the task and method of preaching. The highly personal and fragmentary statements which he has scattered through his writings, stand in sharp contrast to Erasmus' *Ecclesiastes,* the handbook of humanism on Christian rhetoric, which follows the tradition of antiquity and by this dependence loses its understanding of the uniqueness of the Christian sermon. In all of his statements, both in the second series of lectures on the Psalms (1519-1521) and in the table talk, Luther has only thought of preaching as the oral task of presenting the tidings of salvation. To present the word in this way is a terrifying responsibility since this word according to Luther is quietly reverenced by the whole creation. No person, before or since, has so exalted the word, not only the written word, but the living word on the lips of the preacher: "The New Testament office is not written on dead tablets of stone, instead it is entrusted to the sound of living speech." [3] He makes a great many apt observations concerning his own and others' sermons and gives good and often humorous advice to inexperienced recruits to the work. Most basically, however, we receive a sharp impression of how deeply personal was his own relationship to the task. The preacher must present the message and preach to the glory of God, even though there seems to be no fruit: "my preaching is like the man who sings in the woods; he sings for the trees, but only the echo answers." Nevertheless preaching must address people, it must tear down their pride by means of the law, it must comfort the bleeding consciences through the gospel. One phrase may therefore be sufficient for preaching since it can be

---

[3] E. Hirsch (ed.), *Predigten* ("Luthers Werke in Auswahl," Vol. VII [Bonn, 1932]), p. 3. Compare p. 24 where the English equivalent of the Latin is, "To arouse one conscience is greater than to have a hundred kingdoms."

a sufficient channel for the fullness of the whole of Scripture. Luther exerted himself to use only one passage and to stay with it so that it might be said that the sermon really concerned itself with this passage. As a result all technique, all reference to artistic form is subsidiary. He leaves all inherited methodology behind: "Christ has spoken in the most simple way and yet he was eloquence personified (*eloquentia*)—Therefore the highest eloquence is to speak simply (*eloquentia simpliciter dicere*)."[4] To be faithful to the subject is about the only prescription that Luther gives. The preacher must be careful lest he becomes like servant girls who, on the way to the market place, stop and converse with all the acquaintances they meet—"Preachers who wander too far from their subject are doing the same thing. They intend to say everything at once but this is impossible."

Freedom from all the restraints of methodology is the only method Luther used in his own preaching. When later Lutheran theologians discovered that they could speak about *methodus heroica,* the heroic method, as the method which was used by Luther, it was only another way of saying that he could not be fitted into the usual homiletical categories. Even in Luther's preaching, however, it is certainly possible to isolate some of the elements which are found in all preaching, exposition and application of the text. Yet those elements are so often intertwined with each other that it is hardly possible to differentiate them in an orderly manner. The introduction may be completely absent or it may consist of a few short observations on the text. The conclusion often appears very abruptly: the speaker stops when he thinks he has said enough. Sometimes we detect what seems to be a theme or at least a rubric such as a sermon for Sexagesima, "Four Disciples of the Word." Sometimes divisions are given—but all this is quite beside the point. The use of the text changes in accordance with the nature of the text. The

[4] Ibid., p. 35.

111

historic passages are used as supports for faith and as examples for living, and only finally does the mystical interpretation sometimes appear. The didactic texts, especially the Epistle lessons, are often treated purely homiletically so that the exposition proceeds verse by verse. Luther's preaching really consists only of a series of consecutive fragments, many or few, by which he presents all that he considers suitable to the occasion, and by which he attempts through a very free use of the text to make the one gospel of the righteousness of faith speak. In addition, his enthusiasm in combating the doctrine of good works and the false service of God enunciated by the papists, continually tempted him to digress from his subject.

Most German treatments of Luther's preaching have degenerated to the level of an uncritical hero worship. An historical evaluation cannot ignore the obvious weaknesses, among which the neglect of form and the lack of discipline in the arrangement are the most obvious. A more rigid form would, however, not have been consonant with its spontaneous impetuosity which calls to mind a rushing spring torrent, and which gives Luther's preaching its epochal significance.

Prophecy and the Interpretation of Scripture

His disdain for form belongs to the prophetic character of Luther's proclamation. No previous teacher of the church was overpowered by a consciousness of being entrusted with a special message as was Luther. At this point it is impossible to separate his preaching from his other work: both are dominated by the same strong awareness of divine calling. One of the essential characteristics of prophetic preaching is that it is a deed or an act. Luther was conscious of his relationship to the Old Testament prophets. Consequently, in a lecture on Isaiah in the year 1527, he tells how the prophets were given the responsibility of awakening the people to an expectation of the coming Messiah: "Thus it is also the aim of all that we preach and prescribe in the church, that the people shall expect the Savior's coming." Otherwise, however, his prophetic task consisted mainly in presenting the evangel of the Savior who had already come. The preacher's special concern is to set forth this message in any way he can. Luther's affinity to his own age arises out of this context and makes his preaching an historical document of uncommon worth. This is most specifically true of the catechetical addresses and especially the earlier sermons on the Decalogue. The urgent desire to penetrate, to be understood, which is the basic cause for the simplicity of his form, also arises out of this context. He who is able to teach *simpliciter et pueriliter et populanter et trivialiter* ("as simply and as childishly and as popularly and as commonly") as is possible—he is the best preacher. In the pulpit he does not want to think about Bugenhagen, Justus Jonas, and Melanchthon: "I do not preach to them but to little Hans and little Elsa; it is about them I am thinking." The pedagogical element of the sermon stands in the service of the prophetic element. Both the genius-like simplicity and the sometimes tiresome monotony are thus rooted in the consciousness of being entrusted with one errand. This sense of urgency has also left its imprint on the form and has given it a beauty which is primarily dependent on its sense of reality. Many illustrations have disappeared even though isolated instances could be cited where they remain. Symbolic language is used within very narrow limits and very seldom is allowed to blossom forth. The willingness to use personal experiences as illustrations belongs to the prophetic consciousness of the call. The opposition which faced him in the task which had been entrusted to him became the occasion for giving sarcasm and polemic a free— sometimes all too free—rein.

The prophet was aware that it was his responsibility to be a teacher of the Holy Scriptures. It was as a doctor *in sacra pagina* that Luther began to preach. The exegetical character is also inseparably related to the prophetic. Sometimes he could surely, as in the Invocavit sermons, preach without a text, but this was an exception. His preaching was anchored in the pericopes and especially the Gospels, and as a result he made his own contribution to the preservation of this churchly custom. But most preferably he preached on the Epistles where doctrine was explicitly stated. The opportunity for this type of preaching presented itself especially in the weekday sermons. In this connection he expounded whole books of the Bible from the pulpit to a lesser extent than did many of his contemporaries and predecessors. Instead he did this from the professor's desk. In scholarly studies of Luther's work as a textual expositor the sermons have, for this reason, been given a subordinate position to the lectures. But a similar development may be noted in both instances: both as a preacher and as a lecturer, Luther began with the medieval conception of a fourfold meaning of Scripture, but step by step he freed himself from this allegorical method of interpretation. It is nevertheless striking to how high a degree the allegorical method left its imprint even on the older sections of the church postil, where Luther often followed Augustine's example and went for "a spiritual walk." We may well ask the question, what edification did pious readers of Luther receive from such passages as the preposterous mystical speech in the church postil's exposition of the age of Anna the prophetess in a sermon on the Sunday after Christmas?

Even though Luther was led bit by bit to a higher appreciation of *literalis sensus,* the literal meaning, he freed himself only slowly from the tradition of allegorical interpretation. He uses this method as a means of overcoming contradictions in Scripture and as a symbolic method of expression, even as it was used by the earlier saints. But he seeks a spiritual rather than an allegorical interpretation and sometimes this comes closer to the real meaning than the grammatical exposition does. One

114

must seek the basic thought of the text, its *scopus*. This conception was derived from Aristotle and through Luther's influence it again began to be used both in preaching and in the interpretation of Scripture. In this way Luther protected himself against being imprisoned in the narrow literalistic faith which later expressed itself in the orthodox doctrine of verbal inspiration.

Basic for Luther's whole view of the Bible is the notion of the unitary message of salvation which is proclaimed in all Scripture. This proved to be a fruitful approach for all later biblical interpretation, but at the same time it hindered Luther from arriving at a real understanding of the various stages of revelation. When he found the whole scope of the Bible in the Pauline gospel of sin and grace and justification by faith alone, he construed this as a part of every text, even the texts from the Psalms where the author refers to his own righteousness. In these texts Luther thought he found valuable testimonies to the incapability of works as the ground of salvation. Yet at the same time, this, his understanding of the gospel brings with it a clear view of the contrasts between the old and the new covenant, between law and gospel, and gives him a basis for evaluation which also makes it possible to acknowledge the varying worth of the different books of the New Testament. He dares *urgere Christum contra scripturam,* urge Christ in contrast to the Scriptures. At the same time that Scripture is the objective, once-and-for-all message concerning God's acts, where the dark passages must be interpreted with the help of those that are clear, it is also true that its meaning is unveiled only to him whose inner ear has been opened to its spiritual content. This teaching concerning the transformation which is necessary in order that a man might rightly understand the word, introduces, if you will, a subjective principle in the exposition of the objective message. In this way Luther led scriptural interpretation beyond the medieval and humanistic pedantic proclamation of the law of Christ. As none of his predecessors, Luther dealt with the fundamental problems of biblical interpretation, problems with which theology forever continues to wrestle. And here, as in other instances, contradiction and lack of logical sequence is the price which the reformer must pay in order to be able to enter into the real depths of spiritual knowledge, depths which must remain hidden from the mind which works purely logically. Even though his interpretation of Scripture does suffer from obvious weaknesses, he has, nevertheless, indicated the basic lines of development for the continuing penetration of the word of Scripture, a task which continues to be basic for evangelical theology. And even though his textual exposition is far from being exemplary he has still burned into the mind of every evangelical preacher the consciousness that preaching must be an exposition of Scripture. Furthermore, he has related the homiletical explanation of Scripture to Scripture's own central message and addressed it sharply to mankind: for it is only when Scripture speaks to the heart of man, judging and raising him up, that it becomes a living word of God.[5]

Preaching and the Service

Luther's understanding of the place of preaching in the cult hardly ripened to a position of complete clarity. At different times he expressed varying viewpoints. As early as his first essay on the service, "Concerning the Order of the Service in the Congregation" (1523), he expressed the judgment that one of the great weaknesses of the Roman service was that the word of God was not given its rightful status. He then wished to find a place for preaching in the daily service. In the sung matins as well as at vespers, the liturgical responses were to make way

[5] Cf. Willem Jan Kooiman, *Luther and the Bible,* trans. John Schmidt (Philadelphia: Fortress Press, 1961).

116

for the exposition of Scripture. Both morning and evening a passage of Scripture was to be read and explained. When it was intended that the whole Bible should be considered consecutively, primacy was given to the Old Testament, mainly because it took a longer time to read. Sermons were to be preached on the Gospel at mass on Sunday and usually on the Epistle at vespers, but the preacher also had the choice of treating a book of the Bible consecutively. Later Luther also presented a more detailed prescription for the order of lections at the services during the week. In spite of the sharp criticism which Luther could direct against isolated texts, he held fast with a singular stubbornness to the pericopes both as liturgical lections and as preaching texts for the various Sundays. Thus he also retained the sermon in its traditional setting in the mass. In the *Formula Missae* (1523) he certainly suggests that the sermon could also be delivered before the introit. This would be appropriate since the gospel is a voice crying in the wilderness which calls the unfaithful to faith. In his own practice, however, he held fast to the tradition he found in Wittenberg and delivered his Sunday sermons following the creed. He also prescribed the same practice in the *Deutsche Messe* (1526) and in this way established a practice which has been continued in Lutheran Christendom until the present time. Here he also gives good reason for a retention of the pericopes as a guarantee against lack of discipline in the preacher. Spirit-filled preachers who can successfully preach through a whole book are few and far between. In the same way that he retained the church year, after certain specific days had been discarded, Luther also followed this order in his postils. The very name "postil" refers at this point to medieval tradition.

In other respects Luther's extant sermons show very slight traces of the liturgical order into which they were inserted. References to the sentences of the mass or to other cultic motifs are to be sought in vain. The great holidays were occasions for special articles of faith to be expounded such as Christmas Day, "the lofty article concerning the divinity of Christ," or Pentecost, the third of the articles of faith. They did not, however, provoke the same exuberant jubilation which had set its stamp on the preaching of the ancient church on these festival days. The preservation of the church year and the pericopes did, however, have a far-reaching significance since it gave later Lutheran preaching the unique pattern by which it differentiates itself to a great extent from practically all other Christian preaching. "The postil" came into being on Lutheran soil and became the classic form for collections of sermons and devotional books. It is essentially true that to the extent Luther oriented his preaching liturgically, the liturgy continued to be a living resource for Lutheran Christendom.

After Luther

With the exception of the external connections which are created by the pericopes and the church year, it is difficult to find an organic relation between the Reformation itself and later Lutheran preaching. Luther's contribution was of basic significance for the status of preaching in the cult and as no other he raised up the requirement for a tireless proclamation of the word of God. Sometimes we gain the impression of an almost magical conception of the inherent power of the word: if the word is allowed rightly to become current then the blessed result shall not fail to appear. Luther gave rich sources of inspiration to all evangelical preaching but he did this to a lesser degree in his actual homiletical production than by his total influence. His influence upon Lutheran preaching in the centuries that followed immediately after his death was, however, insignificant.

The weakness of this influence depended to a degree on the

fact that, in the tremendous movement which makes up the Reformation, many other elements were also present. The boundary between Lutheran and Reformed church life was only established gradually. South German Lutheranism, of which Johann Brenz (1499-1570) is the most typical representative, did have many points of contact with the Swiss Reformation and also exercised an influence in Scandinavia which sometimes placed Wittenberg in a secondary position. Humanism was a very significant influence within both the system of public education and the theological faculties. Yet the basic reason for Luther's meager influence as a preacher was certainly his contempt for all technique. "The heroic method" was hardly usable by the average preacher whose problem was how to gather material for all the preaching that was demanded of him and to shape it into usable form. The search for a new method thus emerged as the sharpest issue in the development of Lutheran preaching. In this way preaching was led from Luther's formlessness to the opposite extreme.

This development has hardly been given sufficient attention. Recent Lutheran homiletical historians have not been able to see anything but a continuing decline. The contrast between the creation of genius and of routine mechanics is often painfully apparent. But the craftsman also demands recognition. The development of technique is an especially interesting chapter in the history of preaching, even though this chapter has often been ignored. The growth of a new technique is especially apparent in the Lutheran church in the centuries following Luther. Recent evaluations of this development are very unsatisfactory, since they cannot disassociate themselves from a certain tendency to ridicule the theoretical efforts of orthodoxy in this area. To altogether too high a degree they have emphasized the exaggerations, such as the too highly forced schematizing or the naive desire to make the whole more involved than it actually is. Because of this bias, they have been hindered from doing full justice to the intensive work, which was really performed to create a usable homiletical method which could put the average member of the great army of preachers in a position to discharge his responsibility. Such great care has hardly ever been devoted to the technique of preaching and the results are by no means to be despised. To discover how the medieval tradition again reappears is of no little interest. In like manner we can trace a clear connection between the late Middle Ages and fully developed Lutheranism in such other areas as devotional literature and the contemplation of the passion. Here also, orthodoxy was dependent upon Scholasticism. A careful investigation would be necessary to give a detailed explanation of how this happened. The resemblance between the Dominican "art of preaching" and much of the methodology of the seventeenth century is in many respects striking. The correspondences surely depend in part on the fact that in both instances the categories of Aristotelian logic were used. Beyond this, however, we must acknowledge a direct dependence.

The preachers who belonged to Luther's immediate circle of disciples showed only slight traces of the developing emphasis on method. Several of them stood so sharply in the shadow of the reformer that their individual traits did not appear with sufficient clarity. An exhaustive investigation would be desireable at this point. In the innermost circle Johann Bugenhagen (1485-1558) is most significant even though Luther did not deny himself the privilege of joking about his long sermons. Bugenhagen exerted a wide influence on the first generation of Lutheran preachers and contributed to the traditional usage of the appointed pericopes by his handbook on the Gospel lections. We have already met Veit Dietrich (1506-1549), who was very close to Luther personally, as the very arbitrary editor of the house postil. He was one of the most influential exponents of the Greek classical tradition. His manhood years were spent in Nuremberg where his postil for children was produced. Urbanus

Rhegius (1485-1541), a humanist who perhaps basically and ultimately found it difficult to orient himself to his new spiritual environment, bequeathed to posterity one of the first attempts to give theoretical instructions on the art of preaching on Lutheran soil. His work was entitled *Formulae Caute Loquendi* ("Some Ways of Speaking Carefully") and was first published in 1535. Johannes Mathesius (1504-1568), who left behind him a very rich production, was the most original of Luther's disciples. Two of his collections have attained a classic position. *Sarepta,* or "Mountain Postil," a book of homilies intended to explain stories, sayings, and examples in Scripture which mention mining, represents a unique homiletical type. It does, perhaps, refer to the tradition of the Middle Ages. We can be more certain when we make this affirmation about his sermons on the life of Luther, a sort of counterpart to the old sermons on the saints, which have been significant and basic in the creation of the traditional picture of the Reformer, a picture which critical research has found it necessary to revise. Naturally neither collection consists of sermons on the pericopes, since, in keeping with medieval custom, they were delivered during Lent. The Swabian Johann Brenz was more significant than most of the others of the theological tradition. His diligent preaching, which fills a whole row of folio volumes, consisted mainly of a continuous textual exposition. His legacy lies in systematically constructed sermons with a theme and divisions, as well as notes on the Epistle lessons. His place in the history of preaching merits more careful scrutiny.

The history of Lutheran preaching until the latter part of the seventeenth century must deal less with individual contributions than with task and method. In order to be fair to the era we must also reckon with the enormous extensiveness of preaching activity. There has hardly ever been so much preaching as there was during the sixteenth century and during the period of orthodoxy. Services during the week were added to the

Sunday services and bit by bit these services shed the outer pattern of the canonical offices and were given the spoken word as their essential content. Many other occasions could be celebrated with spiritual oratory. Above everything an honorable funeral required much preaching: in this respect also, the development is partly a return to the Middle Ages. Probably the funeral address was used to fill the vacuum which arose because of the disappearance of the office for the dead and the funeral mass. In keeping with an earlier custom of celebrating masses for the dead, preaching services on the eighth and thirteenth day after the burial were observed in addition to the actual funeral and its sermon. A great many types of occasional preaching were also created.

Furthermore, the catechetical sermon retained its place in Lutheran church practice. During the sixteenth century and even into the seventeenth, an almost unlimited need for instruction existed and a no less necessary ethical guidance was added to the theoretical presentation of the main outlines of the faith. The preacher became a schoolmaster and a watchman of morals: the pedagogical motif asserted itself with a strength that is reminiscent of the Carolingian era. Alongside the sermons on the pericopes and the sermons based on whole books of the Bible the catechetical sermon asserted its own claims. It was, however, just as significant that all preaching assumed an educational character. To apply lessons out of the text became the highest homiletical art. Polemics was combined with catechetical preaching, and gained an increasing prominence in direct proportion to the growth of the number of controversial issues; a no less conscious antagonism towards the Reformed orientation was added to the old opposition to the papacy. Finally, and not least important, struggles between various dogmatic schools appeared on Lutheran soil during the period of the writing of the symbols, a period which ended with the appearance of the Formula of Concord (1577). All of these influences contributed to the growth of preaching material. Even though the fact that preaching must be scriptural exposition was never forgotten, the words of Scripture were often used primarily as foundations for the preacher's doctrine, or as weapons against other thought patterns.

Humanism and the Neo-Scholastic Method

The disdain which has been heaped upon that period in the history of Lutheran preaching which concentrated on the development of technique has made it a period that is very obscure and difficult to survey. The confused pattern of the internal history of the German territorial churches also appears, when viewed from the standpoint of homiletical development, as an impenetrable thicket. We can merely attempt to clarify the most important tendencies. Perhaps the main lines are simpler than most interpreters have thought. Students who become seriously acquainted with some of the handbooks which were actually in use will be surprised to learn they are more sensible than current impressions are apt to allow. This is true of a work by H. J. Hülsemann (1602-1661), the well-known handbook *Oratoricae Ecclesiasticae liber unus* ("Book One of Ecclesiastical Oratory"), published in Wittenberg in 1633, as well as one which is less well known but very enlightening, *Methodus Concionandi* ("Method of Public Speaking," Jena 1666) by Christian Chemnitz (d. 1666). It is also true to some extent of the elder Carpzov's *Hodegeticum* ("An Exegetical Guide").[8] There are also good reasons for accepting the fact that popular

___

[8] John Benedict Carpzov the Elder (1607-1657) published a homiletical handbook in 1656 under this title. This work was enlarged by his son, J. B. Carpzov the Younger (1639-1699) in an edition from the year 1689. The latter presents one hundred outlines for one and the same text and is therefore generally considered the culmination of an age of frenzied attention to preaching technique.

preaching appeared in a more simple and popular form than the methods and Latin outlines seem to indicate. This is very evident in a postil by the Saxon court preacher Martin Mirus (1532-1593) published posthumously in 1614. It contains sermons with a clear and simple construction. The text is followed by an exposition which develops into an outline with two or three divisions which are further expanded. It is very surprising to find extremely involved Latin outlines at the end of the volume, arranged in the usual graphic form, but corresponding exactly to the very simple sermons which appear in the volume. A weakness for a display of learning was once again a characteristic of the age. The multiplication of techniques is perhaps also due to this fact. As the methods were developed in the seventeenth century they were often named after various universities, just as the *artes* were in the Middle Ages. Closer study would, perhaps, show these to be relatively insignificant variations of the common basic type.

The question is, how had this basic type come into existence? Certain fundamental factors are very evident. The humanistic influences, which were dependent on the rhetoric of antiquity and Augustine's *De Doctrina Christiana,* were mediated by Melanchthon. He did not appear as a preacher but he did exercise a wide influence through his textbook on rhetoric, *De Officiis Concionatoris* ("Concerning the Office of Public Speaking"), 1535,[7] and through his postil which is best described as a series of

---

[7] As early as 1519, Melanchthon published a short treatise which gives attention to preaching, *De Rhetorica libri tres* ("Three Books on Rhetoric"), which was reissued in 1531 under the title *Elementorum rhetorices libri duo* ("Two Books on the Elements of Rhetoric"). To the three classic *genera causarum* (types of treatment), the *demonstrativum* ("explanatory"), *deliberativum* ("meditative"), and *judiciale* ("judicial"), Melanchthon in 1531 added a fourth, the *didascalicum* ("didactic"), which he describes as the proper *genus* of the sermon. This shows the difficulty of finding a place for the sermon within the inherited categories of rhetoric. It is also an exhibit of the one-sidedly didactic view of the homiletical task which is found in humanism. Melanchthon also differentiated three types of texts and sermons:

lectures on the pericopes in which the pericopes' problems and homiletical possibilities are discussed. The custom of extracting certain lessons, *loci* or *articuli,* from the text stems from Melanchthon. It has therefore been customary to speak about an "articulated" method as the earliest in Lutheran homiletics.[8] All subsequent preachers in this era sought to draw certain *loci* or *doctrinae* out of their texts. To the same extent that a complete partition became customary, every section was often given its own group of *doctrinae.* It later became customary to class Aegidius Hunnius (1550-1603) as a representative of the "articulated" method.

This stream borders upon another which is usually considered as having come from the Dutch Reformed theologian Andreas Gerhard of Ypres (1511-1564), later active in Marburg. He is usually called Hyperius and is classed as the first proper theoretician of the evangelical sermon. Through him a strong dose of humanistic rhetoric also entered the homiletical tradition. He busies himself especially with the antique terms. In common with other speakers the preacher has the threefold task to teach, to delight and to influence—*docere, delectare, flectere.* He gives the basic scheme of division which in the main has been used since that time. The sermons shall contain these

didacticum ("teaching"), *epitrepticum* ("convincing") and *paraeneticum* ("hortatory").

[8] In 1572, one of Melanchthon's disciples, Andrew Pancratius (d. 1576) published a *Methodus Concionandi* ("Methods of Public Speaking") which was given wide circulation. In this work the humanistic orientation, or burden, is dominant. The treatise is basically an attempt to apply the technique of profane rhetoric to the sermon. Pancratius develops four *genera causarum* ("types of treatment"). Of these, only *didascalicum* ("teaching") and *deliberativum* ("meditation") are considered as belonging to spiritual oratory. We should especially notice the meager attention that is given to the text. The sections which an address must contain in accordance with the laws of classical rhetoric are applied to preaching: *narratio* is replaced by the text, *propositio; confirmatio* and *confutatio* are grouped together as a section, *doctrina.* Pancratius thus recommends four divisions: *exordium, doctrina, applicatio* and *peroratio.*

parts: the reading of Scripture, invocation (*invocatio*), introduction (*exordium*), announcement of subject and divisions (*propositio sive divisio*), treatment of the subject (*confirmatio*), argumentation (*confutatio*), conclusion (*conclusio*). This basic scheme has very obvious points of contact with the division which we met in the medieval *artes,* even though the *exordium* is there called the *antethema* and is placed before the text. Soon it also assumed the same position in Lutheran homiletics. Hyperius, however, energetically emphasized the exegetical task in preaching and derived a principle from two passages of Scripture which would be of far-reaching influence in homiletical theory in the subsequent centuries. In II Tim. 3:16 ff. we read, "All Scripture is inspired by God and profitable for teaching, for reproof, for correction, and for training in righteousness." Did not one have here the basic contours of the Bible's own homiletics? He combined this with a passage on the value of Scripture, Romans 15:4, "For whatever was written in former days was written for our instruction, that by steadfastness and by the encouragement of the scriptures we might have hope," and so arrived at the fivefold use of Scripture, which from the time of Hyperius became one of the most cherished techniques in evangelical homiletics. In these passages he thought he had found a basis for the division of the texts into five categories, which were usually given Greek names, according as their basic content consisted of teaching, rebuttal, training, correction, comfort. This basis of division also gained a foothold in the purely Lutheran sermon but here it was changed to the fivefold application. If possible, every sermon ought to draw out of every text this whole series of applications. This is the well known *usus quintuplex* ("the fivefold application").

The material with which orthodoxy's homiletics later busied itself was procured in this way. We find it in varying usages in a long series of homiletical handbooks. To the basic material we may possibly add the increasing emphasis which gradually was given to the *exordium* as an independent section of the sermon. The *exordium* showed a tendency towards expansion at the expense of the other sections of the sermon. Sometimes a threefold *exordium* was prescribed, but at such times an independent character was given the short transitions from text to subject and also to the divisions. We also notice a growing tendency to unite the various *loci* into a unified theme just as in the Scholastic sermon. The seventeenth century was, however, less formally biblical than the Middle Ages; in orthodoxy the theme did not need to be a passage of Scripture, in the synthetic sermon it rather became a dogmatic *locus*. The history of the theme in Lutheran preaching needs more careful research.

The history of the orthodox preaching technique is an extensive and very confusing chapter. Here research could be assigned the task, which is by no means uninteresting, of investigating how the various lines of development are intertwined. In *Methodus Concionandi,* referred to above, Christian Chemnitz offered a moderate example of the fully developed technique. Here he summarized all earlier methods of preaching in four categories: the heroic—Luther's own method, the paraphrastic, the articulated, and the thematic. He found that these may again be traced back to two basic types, the analytic or paraphrastic and the synthetic. Of these he, himself, preferred the analytic since the treatment of the text could easily become "arbitrary and forced" when the synthetic method was used.

A study of Chemnitz' presentation leaves a very favorable impression of practical moderation. To be sure, we do find a discussion of the question as to whether or not the divisions of the theme should be expressed in rhyming Latin phrases; we surely also find the old well-known rhetorical cliches, such as the view that the *exordium* is to "prepare good will, attention and willingness to learn." The presentation concerning *inventio,* the gathering of material, dates back to Augustine. There are, however, many accurate observations and wise words of counsel.

This is especially true of his textual analysis. The text certainly has the specific task of buttressing the subject. Chemnitz does, however, warn against basing a subject on one word in the text; it must be derived from the text and not be superimposed upon it. We must give attention to the orderliness and the context of the text. Suggestions for different kinds of textual analysis are always worthy of consideration. The orthodox preachers did not shun energetic work with the text, and the homileticians gave much attention to perfection of the instruments which could be used in this task. Chemnitz prefers, as we have pointed out earlier, the paraphrastic method over the thematic, but the paraphrastic method also requires a subject and a systematic arrangement. The *exordia* should be short and delivered in a moderate tone, "the speaker must grow while he speaks." *Propositio,* which is basically the same as the theme, may be simple or composite. Among the theoreticians of orthodoxy we hardly ever find any absolute requirement for a unified theme, although the general development does move in the direction of a firmer formulation of a subject. *Confirmatio* becomes the main section and here the emphasis is on *elaboratio doctrinarum,* the development of the various doctrinal teachings arising out of the text. *Confutatio,* the argumentation, a section which actually has its home in the oratory of antiquity, hardly ever occurs in preaching. In Chemnitz' treatise we meet a reminder of *pathologia* as an important chapter in homiletics. Hülsemann has also given an exhaustive treatment of the subject. The intent is so to use the word of the Bible and other homiletical material that the mood of the hearers is purposefully influenced.

Techniques and Helps

A direct confrontation with a few of the most-used handbooks from the seventeenth century awakens the suspicion that the traditional presentation of the Lutheran theory of preaching in the seventeenth century is altogether too stereotyped and somewhat unjust. There was, to be sure, onesideness and exaggeration in the seventeenth century's homiletical output. The twenty-six methods of preaching which were defined by J. Föster are surely expressions of a learned pedantry which depresses, but to this curiosity altogether too much attention has been given. German homiletics of the late nineteenth and early twentieth centuries viewed the seventeenth century through glasses colored by pietism and noted such extravagances with special relish.[9] Various kinds of aberrations and excesses were found. The purely mechanical task of analyzing and arranging was given such emphasis that formal matters became the principal concern. It is plain that we need a more just critical analysis.

In this context we must give specific attention to the interesting question of relationships to medieval homiletics. The parallels are evident. This is especially true in respect to the creation of the tremendous collections of material for the use of the preacher. J. S. Adami's *Deliciae evangelicae oder evangelische Ergotzlichkeiten* ("The Charm of the Gospel" or "The Delightfulness of the Gospel"), to be sure, began to be published in 1704 but the volumes are, nevertheless, a typical example of this extensive literature. With its fifteen volumes it is a Protestant counterpart to John of Bromyard's *Summa.* In it preachers could find not only scholarly analyses of the days and the texts, but also illustrations and subject arrangements which were more or less artificial. The use of illustrations is also a characteristic which reminds us of the Middle Ages. Here we can also consider the many narratives found in *Seelenschatz* ("The Treasure of the Soul") by Christian Scriver (1629-1693), a work describing the

---

[9] This seems to be especially true of the work of R. Rothe, M. Schian, and E. C. Achelis. In Schian's valuable treatise from 1912, *Orthodoxie und Pietismus im Kampf um die Predigt,* there is an attempt objectively to evaluate the pietistic critique of orthodox preaching, yet even this attempt remains basically determined by the pietistic outlook.

progress of the soul from misery to eternal life and combining allegory, dogmatics and ethics. Material from the collections of the Middle Ages sometimes came into use again. We must view the emblematic method, which is generally classed as one of the aberrations of later orthodoxy, as also arising out of this context. Here we are referring to the fully developed metaphorical sermon, which on occasion assumed bizarre forms; for example, a Saxon court preacher is said to have preached during a whole church year on "God's Tower," alluding to well-known buildings with towers in Dresden and using three divisions: God's Powder Tower, God's Castle Tower, and God's Cross Tower. Another of Saxony's homiletical geniuses is said to have spoken a whole year on Jesus as an artisan (Jesus the best paperhanger, etc.). These preachers were only following a medieval tradition, which reached typical expression in the motif of the chess game as used in morality plays, where every man and every move was given a spiritual meaning, and in the exposition of *Castellum religionis* with its moat, its drawbridge, its tower, and its defenders. The same type of homiletical activity also emerged in Roman Catholic preaching in the seventeenth century, preaching which also exhibits other points of contact with Lutheran scholasticism.

Homiletical theorizers were by no means negligent in taking suggestions from their Reformed or Roman Catholic colleagues. The artificiality evident in the preaching of the latter part of the seventeenth century merely reflects the general esthetic tendency current in all forms of literary production. The preference for pomposity, and for the curving and swelling forms which are characteristic of baroque architecture and poetry, also left its imprint on preaching. When, for example, Adamis suggests "Mary as a singing, beautiful nightingale" as the subject for the Fifteenth Sunday after Trinity or suggests to his preachers that they speak on "The Lord Jesus' Farewell Cantata" (with two divisions: its beginning in B major; its conclusion in B minor) on Cantate, the Fourth Sunday after Easter, the spirit is in harmony with the chubby-cheeked cherubs which decorated the baroque church buildings.

Churchmen in no other era have given the technical problems of preaching such intensive attention as did the Lutherans in the seventeenth century, the era of hundreds of postils and innumerable methods. An unbiased judge must recognize both honesty of purpose and persistent concern. The demand for homiletical productions was enormous and only an abnormally high technique could possibly satisfy the need. Rigorous adherence to the use of the pericopes at the regular Sunday services presented certain special problems. It was the special problem of giving variety to the treatment of the same text that gave the *exordium* its distinctive place in Lutheran homiletics. If we wish to see this formal technique of preaching reach its climax we may turn to J. B. Carpzov the Younger (1639-1699). In 1689 he edited a new edition of his father's homiletical handbook, *Hodegeticum*, with added notations. In this collection he gives one hundred different examples for treating a single short text from the Psalms (Ps. 14:7). Even though it is customary to speak of Carpzov's hundred methods as the high point in the methodological frenzy, this is a judgment which depends on a mistake which hardly would have been passed along, if scholars had taken the trouble to consult the original source. Though the methodical treatment has surely been given as much variety as possible, the variation has been produced mainly by the use of different *exordia*. Here we have an example of the tendency, very usual in later Lutheran preaching, to let the *exordium* be more dominant than the text. Even though the hundred methods are thus a fiction, we do, nevertheless, feel very depressed by this example of homiletical acrobatics. The author lets us know that he could easily produce another hundred sermon outlines. Carpzov's *Artis concionatoriae tyrocinium*[10] is,

[10] The English equivalent of the whole Latin title would read as follows: "An exhibit of the various methods of preaching together with

131

however, more illuminating for homiletic technique than the *Hodegeticum*. Here the Sunday pericopes are treated to assist the inexperienced "recruits." An analytic outline and a synthetic outline are given for every text. The *genus* (type) of the text is first of all established—the Gospel for the Fourth Sunday in Advent (John 19:1-28) is judged as belonging to *genus didascalicum,* the type of teaching. In the treatment according to the analytic method, the *exordium* is taken from Psalm 119 and the logical division contains three main parts.[11] The *propositio* is "concerning the testimony of John the Baptist" and this subject is divided so as to refer to his steadfastness, his zeal, his office. Following a short *votum* every part is considered in turn and further divided with added *loci communes* (passages treating the general topic), which is equivalent to the fivefold scheme's *usus*. Only two of the five types are used, however. The conclusion gives a summary of the *argumenta* in the sermon. The synthetic treatment is no less schematic in its arrangement, than the analytical, but the subject stands in a more free relation to the text without being systematic: *De aurora diei Christi natalitii* ("Concerning the Dawn of the Natal Day of Christ"). The Latin names of the divisions rhyme just as in the Middle Ages.[12] We wonder what joy the hearers received from this presentation.

---

two expositions on the pericopes for the entire year for inexperienced preachers" (Leipzig, 1698).

[11] The text for the *exordium*, Ps. 119:46, reads as follows: "I will also speak of thy testimonies before kings, and shall not be put to shame." The divisions are made according to the following scheme: Who is speaking? What does he say? How does he speak?

[12] *Propositio: De aurora diei Christi natilitii, in qua deprehendimus,* I. *Luciferum solem indicantem.* II. *Vocem vigilis suscitantem.* III. *Rorem salubriter humectantem.* IV. *Radium solis emicantem.* ("*Propositio:* Concerning the dawn of the natal day of Christ, on which we apprehend: (1) The light of the morning star appearing; (2) The voice of the watchman being raised up; (3) The salutary dew watering the earth; (4) The rays of the sun breaking forth.")

In Carpzov, technical homiletics not only reached its zenith but developed to the point of absurdity. But even here it is better than its reputation. The homiletics of Lutheran orthodoxy merits treatment with a certain respect because of its noteworthy attempt to come to terms with the problem of preaching from the pericopes. It has created a type which, although usually practiced in a more simplified form, has been decisive for the pattern of tradition-bound Lutheran preaching up to the present time.

Analysis of Orthodoxy's Proclamation

The exceptionally productive era in the history of preaching from Luther's death to the beginning of the eighteenth century cannot be thoroughly analyzed without a closer investigation of its particular details. An attempt at such an evaluation should be made. We immediately gain the impression that the basic sermon elements have been crowded into the background by purely formal and methodical interests. To some degree this depends upon the fact that it is the methodological work which first comes to our attention. If we could arrive at a living picture as to how the method was applied, the impression would, perhaps, change. But doubtless we must emphasize the indisputable fact that the preaching technique itself, during this period as well as during the Middle Ages, and also because of its dependence on the medieval homiletics, emerges as a factor with a status that is too independent to allow it to be dismissed as a minor motif. The sermon which arose as a fruit of the technical interest, should, however, be judged by the same principles that we use to judge other types of preaching.

Rightly to fix the place of the exegetical element in Lutheran orthodoxy's preaching is a very comprehensive task. Ultimately, this is the conclusive question of the use of the Bible in the orthodox theology. No matter to what degree this theology bore the Scholastic and polemical imprint, it nevertheless exhibited its dependence on the Bible as its ultimate foundation. Knowledge of the original biblical languages therefore became the cornerstone in the training of pastors. The doctrine of the nature of the Bible was therefore hammered out as an extreme dogma of inspiration. Most of the handbooks in homiletics rested on the presupposition that preaching must be biblical exposition.

The seriousness with which orthodoxy, in its final phase, gave attention to the interpretation of Scripture is illustrated in a little statement on exegetical method by J. B. Carpzov the Younger. He proposes in *Theologia Exegetica* ("Exegetical Theology," 1701) twelve rules which the preacher must use in his work on the text. An honest piety together with a knowledge of the original languages and the historical background are the most necessary qualifications: the relationship is illuminating. He emphasizes that the literal meaning must first be made clear; only after this can the mystical be investigated. The interpreter must become acquainted with the persons, places, and times, in order to establish the general purpose (*scopus generalis*) of the biblical book as well as the specific purpose (*scopus specialis*) of the appointed pericope. A more careful analysis of details follows this task, after which the meaning of the various words as they occur in other books of the Bible is also investigated. Parallel passages are also given and in accordance with the "analogy of faith," the text is related to the confessional writings. The dogmatic and ethical teachings are drawn from the text and finally the work of other interpreters is used as an aid. We cannot deny that such an energetic exposition of the text as these regulations seem to demand gains our respect. At the same time, it is evident that the process leads to an exaggerated straining of the letter and a one-sided concentration on the isolated passage of Scripture, the pericope, and so that the continuity of revelation is made obscure. This tendency was surely reinforced by the continued practice of binding the Sunday sermon at the morning service to the pericope. The continuous biblical interpretation which was customary during the sixteenth century now became less common. The use of *exordia,* on the other hand, presented an opportunity of including other sections of the Bible, and at many other times when a free choice of texts was given the preachers used selections from the Old Testament.

According to orthodoxy's view of the Bible, every passage of Scripture possessed the same authority and every passage expressed the same revelatory content as the gospel. Now, as in the Middle Ages, Scripture became less a living unity than an inexhaustible storehouse of proof passages, a quiver full of sharp arrows which the knowledgeable homiletician could fit to his bow. The exegetical technique was an exaggerated, virtuoso's juggling of passages which is hardly consonant with real respect for Scripture. Carpzov the Younger is an example of this: his hundred outlines are a journeyman's specimen for master's rank in the skilled trade of using the Bible all too externally. Basic respect for the word of Scripture did not hinder the use of a great deal of additional nonbiblical material in preaching. This especially included dogmatic material, which was derived from the confessional writings, the word of which was sometimes considered equal in inspiration to the word of Scripture. When pietism criticized the one-sidedness of the orthodox preaching and demanded a more biblical and exegetical proclamation it certainly was acting on the basis of good motive. In Philip Jacob Spener (1635-1705), however, the presentation of the doctrine of salvation also became the basic purpose for the exposition of Scripture. Here he found help in the old preaching pattern of orthodoxy, by using the *exordium,* which often became senselessly long, as the occasion for presenting the methodical instruction which could not be included in the exegesis of the pericopes.

The question of the sermon's relation to the liturgy was hardly even real for Lutheran homileticians. Their directions generally were concerned with sermons for special occasions, and churchly custom did offer a large number of such opportunities as supplements to the regular Sunday services. At this juncture we cannot trace the development by which the remaining canonical offices were transformed into preaching services; the handbooks deal primarily with the sermon at morning worship. The characteristic pattern of preaching which was developed during this period—with greater firmness than ever before in the history of the church—was thus to no small degree determined by the setting of the sermon within the context of the liturgy. There were no unnecessary limitations in regard to the sermon's length. The style itself must have been influenced by the somber environment, giving the language of Lutheran preaching its tenacious tendency toward stiff-legged solemnity. The liturgical traits appear most clearly in the attachment to the church year and the pericopes, an attachment which was carried through more rigorously on Lutheran soil than in any other section of the church universal. The Roman Catholic sermon has always claimed a certain right to a free choice of texts and in Reformed Christendom the pericopes have intentionally been abandoned.

In Lutheran preaching the attachment to the pericopes has remained, both as a shackle and as an opportunity. Of late there has been a greater willingness than formerly to admit that this attachment has been of real value. This is especially true of the Swedish church where the attachment has been more firm and where it has continued longer than in any other communion. The retention of the pericopes has continued to be a constitutive characteristic of Lutheran preaching. It has made the "postil" the canonical form for the collection of sermons. It has also made the church year decisive in its influence on the nature of its preaching. The message of the seasons has influenced the spoken word in many respects. In addition to the appointed texts, the traditional hymns for various holidays and seasons of the church year have been an aid and perhaps also a source of inspiration. Not seldom do we find that the old Latin names for the Sundays before and after Easter, *Invocabit, Laetare, Jubilate, Cantate,* have influenced the choice of *exordia* and subjects.

The inner structure of preaching was also influenced by its liturgical environment. This happened negatively by textual restrictions which contributed toward making the *exordium* a constituent part of the sermon, and thus made freedom possible in the selection of the *exordium.* The *exordium* became the means by which the preacher created variation in his use of the perennial texts. The discourse often received its orientation from the *exordium* and the text was often given a subsidiary role. The use of the *exordium* is generally one of the most interesting traits in the pattern of Lutheran preaching. The deed in the pulpit and the sermon itself became a liturgical act. In the Middle Ages, *die offene Schuld* had been such a liturgical addition to the address itself. In the evangelical liturgies this was often replaced by a long prayer to which the congregational announcements were added. The tendency toward the assumption of a liturgical character by the sermon was also evident in the spoken word itself by the use of set introductory and concluding formulas. This had also been the practice in the ancient church. The Lutheran development also included the insertion of one verse of a hymn, sung between the *exordium* and the reading of the text, together with the development of other fixed elements. This is also true of the *votum* which was usually placed after the text and was often constricted into a very rigid pattern. No doubt the tendency toward the schematic, the concern for propositions, the formulation of divisions, and the geometrical exactitude in subject arrangement, all of which were primarily motivated by logic, were also supported by the general tendency toward transforming preaching into liturgy, and this in turn was evoked by the fact that the sermon was set in the context of the service. The seventeenth century is not the only era where we are able to trace the tendency whereby preaching becomes a liturgical rubric.

Noteworthy Individuals

The golden age of homiletical technique left little room for original personal contributions. Although Luther himself is the best example of an essentially prophetic preacher, we must question whether or not this category is generally applicable to Lutheran preaching prior to 1700. It seems as if the mechanics of preaching have excluded direct inspiration. But perhaps here also a careful examination of the sources may lead us to another conclusion.

Orthodoxy's preaching was aware that it had a message for its own time. Even though it is one-sided and constricted, polemic against other confessions and churches is an expression of this awareness. Pedagogical and administrative traits were surely an answer to the crying need for Christian instruction and training. To the degree that Lutheran preaching in the seventeenth century was a concrete and audacious proclamation of the law, it was determined by the demands of its own time to such an extent that the evangelical content of the message was sometimes imprisoned. This trait appears very powerfully in the history of Swedish preaching.

It is, however, strikingly difficult to find preachers who rise above the multitude of sermon manufacturers, and we can only include in the prophetic tradition those who have an unalloyed personal message which they are compelled to utter. A collective prophecy would be an absurdity. In this context we first of all think of Johann Arndt who was born in 1555 and died as general superintendent in Celle, Hanover, in 1621. The independence of his reaction against the quarrelsome enthusiasm of the disciples of pure doctrine, and the seriousness of his demand for a Christianity with more inwardness and immediacy give his gentle personality something of the stature of a prophet. His message, however, came to a great extent from mystical springs, springs that pour their waters into all confessional rivers. Through Arndt's influence, Tauler again, and sometimes very literally, became a subject of conversation. It is the vein of inner, absorbing love for God which has made Arndt's *True Christianity*[13] as well as his *The Garden of Paradise* so beloved by Lutheran Christians in various times. No matter how vehemently the dogmatic rod has attacked Lutheran mysticism, in which fellowship with God is more important than justification, we may nevertheless not contest Arndt's right to a home in Lutheran Christendom unless we wish to rob Lutheranism of some of its comprehensiveness and depth. *True Christianity* was basically a book for edification, and Arndt's sermons, which have been widely distributed, present his viewpoint in a moderate tone. The postil is an interesting example of a moderate and archaic type of Lutheran preaching. The sermons are not based upon a unified subject and, following the very freely constructed *exordium,* two lessons are generally drawn from the text.[14]

Arndt's heir, Heinrich Müller (1631-1675), professor and superintendent in Rostock, may lay claim to prophetic worthiness only to a lesser degree than Arndt himself, even though he represented Christian inwardness with power and seriousness over against a secularized church. In his studied, "emblematic" manner, he exhibits the characteristics of his own age to a remarkable degree. He did exert a tremendous influence as the author of devotional literature, his best known work being "The

[13] Johann Arndt, *True Christianity: a treatise on sincere repentance, true faith, the holy walk of the Christian, etc.,* trans. and ed. A. W. Boehm and Charles F. Schaeffer (Philadelphia: Smith, English & Co., 1868).

[14] The outline for a sermon on the Day of the Transfiguration of Christ is constructed as follows: I. The history of the transfiguration of the holy body of Christ; II. The lessons which this history contains.

Heavenly Kiss of Love" (1659). Christian Scriver (1629-1693), court preacher in Quedlinburg is, however, still more important in this context. His tremendous book *Seelenschatz* (1675-1692) grew out of many years of preaching at weekday services. They are related to the medieval tradition of illustrative sermons (*exempla*) and they passed this tradition on to later low church preachers. Joachim Lütkemann (1608-1655), who died as superintendent in Wolfenbüttel, is to be counted as belonging to the same school of devotional authors. Various influences began to evoke a certain reversal of this current at the end of the seventeenth century. With this development we must reckon with the new streams of cultural life and especially with certain influences from French classicism. The most thoroughgoing homiletical contributions, however, came from the new pietistic movements, which now began to turn their impatient criticism toward the unspiritual preaching of orthodoxy as well as against its dead literalness.

The pietism of Halle surely prepared the way for the dissolution of the orthodox tradition, but in the essentials it adhered to its homiletical pattern. Philip Jacob Spener, who was born in 1635 and who died 1705 as advisor to the consistory and pastor in Berlin, was no prophetic personality. He did not succeed in carrying through the revival of preaching in his own proclamation which he demanded in his *Pia Desideria* (1675).[15] In spite of his serious struggle to make the biblical content living and fruitful, he landed in a schoolmasterish pedantry which made the dust lie thick on his extensive homiletical production. He wished to be a biblical exegete in the spirit of Luther, but basically he belongs rather to the tradition of Reformed exposition. For him, as well as for later pietism's preachers, the requirement of preaching on the pericopes became a heavy armor which became even heavier through his attempt to contain his

[15] Philip Jacob Spener, *Pia Desideria,* trans. and ed. Theodore G. Tappert (Philadelphia: Fortress Press, 1964).

message within this compass. Since the Gospel lessons gave altogether too little place to the specific teachings which he wished to present, he resolved the difficulty by giving the *exordium* an independent status and a didactic pattern. In his absurdly detailed introductions he was thus able to interpret parts of the catechism and entire biblical books, especially the letters of Paul. In its so-called *Exordia Fixa,* pietism's preaching created a unique appendage on the old technical pattern.

Spener did not become a popular preacher, nor did he, like Arndt and Scriver, win readers in various countries. But in spite of the evident formal weaknesses, he introduced a new and impelling motif in preaching by his concentration on sanctification and personal life. The ideas which he himself was not able to execute, in spite of his faithful work, fructified the work of his successors. Biblical depth, practical orientation and missionary enthusiasm, coupled with great talents as a preacher made August Hermann Francke (1663-1727), professor in Halle, the most influential among the preachers of the older pietism. His concern to present, at any cost, what he considered the one central message of Scripture made it possible for him to ignore all rhetorical demands. His sermons, which were not written but presented extemporaneously after meditation, were often painfully long. The collections transcribed by his hearers have been significant even for Swedish piety. A prophetic touch is found in his attempt to make the gospel speak directly to man. Responsibility for active service and especially for missions were also included as part of his preaching and in this manner he widened the sphere of subject matter. In spite of his conscious opposition to orthodoxy's overemphasis on technique, he used the basic style which had developed during the seventeenth century and in this way he contributed toward its preservation in later times. The Halle pietism, in spite of its opposition to the Scholastic technique, finally acted as an agent to conserve the old pattern of preaching.

SIX

An Ecumenical Survey

Variety and richness are inseparably intertwined in more recent eras in the history of the church. It is at one and the same time both a fascinating and a melancholy task to analyze the boundless multiplicity of types of piety and forms of cultic life which have arisen as a result of the Reformation. No doubt, these have their origin to an essential degree in the power of the word that has been made free to create new forms and in the rediscovery of the long-forgotten biblical orientation, but to a degree they are also dependent on the fact that the tremendous process of religious renewal disintegrated the simple greatness of the church of the Middle Ages into its component parts. To study the uniqueness of the churches' various images as it reflected in preaching is very interesting, but it is also a task which is almost wholly untouched. Here we can only make a rough outline of the main tendencies which are discernible in the studies which have been made by contemporary research.

The Roman Catholic Church

In many respects the Reformation exerted a positive influence on the Roman Catholic church. We are, however, not justified in considering the Counter Reformation merely as a symptom of reaction. Unquestionably, it awakened a new interest in the task of preaching. The most striking example of this renewed interest is the famous injunction of the Council of Trent that bishops and parish priests must make provision that sermons be preached in every congregation, at least on all Sundays and holidays, as well as daily during seasons of fasting, or at least three times a week. The new emphasis here is the requirement for preaching on ordinary Sundays, a requirement which was not unknown in the Middle Ages. St. Charles Borromeo (1538-84), Archbishop of Milan and one of the most impressive personalities in the Counter Reformation, made a significant spiritual contribution through his spiritual academy, his own sermons, and his pastoral directives. The fact that the postil, which also is a creation of the Middle Ages, prospered in the Roman Catholic church during the sixteenth century is to some extent dependent upon influences from Lutheran sources. We are reminded of the exposition of the Gospels by John Eck (1486-1543), and of John Wild (1495-1554), the Grey Friar from Mainz, and his German postil. Homiletical expositions on complete books of the Bible, especially the Old Testament books, also appeared as a result of the interest of the Council of Trent in the renewal of preaching. The controversial and polemical sermon flowered in Roman Catholic circles no less than among the evangelicals and this gave added significance to the thematic pattern. In general, work on homiletical technique developed along parallel lines and we surely should be able to show a considerable reciprocal influence. The Spanish preacher, Luis of Granada (1505-1588) used the same genera in his churchly rhetoric, in part the same methods, as the Lutheran homileticians.

Even though the history of Roman Catholic preaching during this period offers a great deal that is of interest, we can by no means speak of a real flowering. The Catholic homileticians themselves acknowledge a period of decline which reaches its lowest point in the seventeenth century. The parochial Sunday sermon to a great extent became only a pious hope. The living proclamation was limited in scope and followed the pattern of the Middle Ages. Perhaps to a greater degree than ever before, preaching was concentrated in the seasons of fasting, primarily

Advent and Lent. More and more the representatives of the orders were given the responsibility of meeting the demands which were placed on the preachers' ability to heighten religious emotion by means of violent rhetorical assaults, assaults which have their counterpart in the Reformed and Free Church revival campaigns of a later era, and which were designed to bring their hearers to repentance. This preaching, however, had no organic place in the cult other than its placement in a specific season of the church year. The text was used as a weapon in the rhetorical attack on the heart of man; not as the source and standard of the proclamation. Many of the weaknesses of the medieval sermon, its fondness for anecdotes, its display of learning and rhetorical bombast, its sometimes burlesque folksiness, appear again in the sixteenth and seventeenth centuries. Abraham a Sancta Clara (Ulrich Megerle, 1644-1709), a discalced Augustinian monk, is one of the most glaring examples of such variants. He won renown as court preacher in Vienna: his large work, *The Arch-Rogue Judas* (1686-95, four volumes), can be classed as one of the most bizarre phenomena in the history of preaching. The "emblematic" method with its fantastic use of symbols flourished in Roman Catholic baroque art and architecture, and its appearance in evangelical preaching was surely partially due to influences from Catholic sources. Catholic preaching was more sharply influenced by humanistic rhetoric than was Lutheran preaching, and at least in equal degree it exhibited the marks both of Scholasticism's passion for homiletical divisions and of spiritual aridity. The satirical novel *Historia del Famoso predicador fray Gerundio de Campazas* ("History of the celebrated preacher Fray Gerundio de Compazas"), 1758, by the Spanish Jesuit José Isla (1703-1781) shows how the preparation of sermons could degenerate into unoriginal copying from the tremendous storehouse of sermons and collections of material. This painful encounter with the degenerate sermon is proof that concern for the preaching of the word was never completely extinguished in the Roman Catholic church. The honor of having maintained this concern belongs especially to the Jesuits.

In contrast to the decline in Spain and the symbolical folly of Abraham a Sancta Clara, the spiritual renaissance in classical France stands even more clearly in bold relief. To some extent we may designate an Italian, Paolo Sagneri, as a precursor of this movement. He also was a Jesuit and he won fame chiefly as a result of his Lenten sermons. Antique rhetoric was renewed and once again made fruitful in Jesuit homiletics. The rhetorical revival was combined with genuinely popular oratory and extensive familiarity with the biblical sources, although one can hardly say that the preaching was consonant with the spirit of the Bible. The foundations for a renaissance of churchly oratory were laid in this manner.

It was in French classicism that this renaissance of preaching burst into full bloom and attained one of its absolutely highest peaks, perhaps not in the history of preaching, but certainly in the history of religious rhetoric. The ecclesiastical oratory, which sought its standards in antiquity, has never come closer to those models than it did during the time of Louis XIV. For the first time in modern history the ecclesiastical art of oratory gained an accepted status in the history of literature. In an era when political absolutism did not provide a place for oratory, rhetoric found a welcome haven of refuge in the pulpit. An analysis of the spiritual oratory of French classicism leads us into the jumble of political, cultural and religious forces which gave this brilliant period its distinctive character. Jansenism left its imprint in the spiritual structure of France even though it was condemned by the church. J. B. Bossuet (1627-1704), the Bishop of Meaux, who usually is rated as the foremost in the famous cloverleaf of court preachers, was the foremost Gallican. Chrysostom and Augustine served as his models. His education, which was primarily determined by humanism and the church fathers, also included a knowledge of the Bible. He gave a great deal of time to biblical study and left behind him a whole shelf of exegetical works. Even as a fifteen-year-old he had been fascinated by the Vulgate: the figurative language of the prophets shows its influence on his style, and we are also able to find in his writings many examples of an ingenious use of texts. Nevertheless, posterity finds it difficult to arrive at a clear understanding of his preaching, and his writings also present some critical literary problems. Bossuet generally wrote his addresses, but in the presentation he often departed from his manuscript, the same manuscript which posterity must use as the basis for an evaluation of his rhetorical art. In his usual appearances as a bishop he generally extemporized on the basis of his highly developed talent for form. His unique reputation as a speaker is based upon the extant carefully constructed funeral orations, *Oraisons funèbres,* the most famous of which is the address on the Prince of Condé. These addresses are a brilliant continuation of the antique tradition of panegyric, which already in the Cappadocian era was transplanted onto Christian soil, but we can hardly class them as sermons. None of the Christian rhetoricians who added luster to the Gallican Byzantium possessed Chrysostom's independence. Bossuet did not, however, personally value the art of spiritual oratory very highly. He saw his own most important responsibility as the fight against moral corruption. He is one of the most brilliant examples of Roman Catholic preaching's traditional struggle against vice, and in the presence of Louis XIV he dared to designate pride as one of the most dangerous sins.

Bossuet's successor as the favorite court preacher was the Jesuit, Louis de Bourdaloue (1632-1704). Louis was a moralist to an even greater extent than his predecessor. His cold severity made an impression on an era which loved clarity. It has been said that the appreciation of Bourdaloue is an honor to the seventeenth century. Posterity finds it more difficult to appreciate him. He disdained artistic patterns and sought to reach the will through the understanding rather than through the emotions. The third preacher in this group, Jean-Baptiste Massillon (1663-1742), Bishop of Clermont, and one who succeeded in making Louis XIV dissatified with himself, lived in a new historical era. His ethical preaching won him Voltaire's approbation as one alongside Confucius and other ethical teachers. He did not possess his predecessors' theological training and mature judgment, and he has been accused of being a secular, rather than a Christian moralist, but he certainly did not lack serious concern for the care of souls. In contrast to Bourdaloue, he addressed the emotions rather than the intellect.

Francois de Fénelon (1651-1715), Archbishop of Cambrai and lofty mystic and pedagogue, stood in conscious opposition to the court preachers of the school of Bossuet. He was a zealous preacher of the word to a greater degree than most of his contemporaries, but only a few sermons from his hands have been preserved for posterity. These, as well as his collection of sermon outlines, *Plans des sermons,* show a clearer understanding of the essential task of preaching than those of the admired rhetoricians who during Lent gave spiritual nourishment to the court. In addition, his discourses "On Oratory, and chiefly on Pulpit Oratory" (*Dialogues sur l'éloquence en general, et sur celle de la chaire en particulier,* Paris, 1718), contain a sound criticism of the abuses and excesses of his contemporaries, especially their altogether too superficial use of the text.

The influence of the French classical sermon was far reaching. It not only included French Reformed preaching in its sphere of influence but extended this influence to every branch of the Christian church during the eighteenth century. In a purely formal sense no other movement has been more significant for the history of preaching in one century. Unquestionably it contributed mightily towards a heightening of the prestige of spiritual oratory since it was not until the nineteenth century that sermons ceased to be classed as literature. But from other perspectives we may raise the question whether or not this influence was sound, whether or not it rather led preaching astray. The great French preachers have been judged and praised primarily for their literary contribution. The purely homiletical investigation of their work remains an uncompleted task. In this compass it is only possible to present two viewpoints.

The tendency to divorce the sermon from its liturgical context, which we have earlier noticed as a characteristic of the Middle Ages, also left its imprint on French classical preaching. We are very poorly informed about the sermon which was delivered at mass during this period. The production of the great orators contains very little of this type of preaching. Besides the panegyrical *oraisons funèbres* the production consists primarily of Lenten sermons. The great goal of the spiritual rhetorician's search for honor and fame was to be summoned to court during Lent. These Lenten sermons were delivered both on ember days during the week and on Sundays, and because of this they treated selected subjects usually without reference to the pericopes. It was in such a series that Massillon recited the duties of the king to the eighty-year-old Louis XV. In this situation they naturally did not abandon their pretensions of being biblical: some of Bossuet's addresses are interlarded with citations from Scripture and are filled with scriptural figures. The word of Scripture occupies a prominent place in Bourdaloue's homiletical arsenal. A Roman Catholic scholar called him "a homiletical strategist" who knew how to use texts and to mobilize their possibilities for his own purposes.[1] The weakness in this biblical usage is at this point apparent. The word of Scripture is a weapon and a means, not a compelling norm. This is also true of Massillon's famous sermon on the rich man, where he is primarily looking for argumentative proof in the text. This method of using the Bible may be an improvement

[1] F. Stingeder, *Geschichte der Schriftpredigt* (1920), p. 165.

148

on pure allegorizing—which appears in this era only as an exception—but it does not satisfy the demand for textual integrity which must be placed upon the Christian sermon. This criticism certainly must also very often be made both of Lutheran and Reformed preaching.

The prophetic orientation cannot be denied. In this respect we must emphasize the address to the times made possible by the special character of the Lenten sermons more than the direct influence of the Old Testament prophets or the purely rhetorical use of Isaiah's figurative language by Bossuet. Massillon's address, *Sur les tentations des grand* ("On the Great Temptations") was not lacking in current interest. These preachers did not stand apart from their own time; their writings are rather the most typical expressions of the uniqueness of their own era. But it is for this very reason that they lose the authentic prophetic quality. Oratory became the servant of royal politics, especially church politics, and the ethical exhortation was often attuned to the note that appealed to the ears of the noble audience. At other times the preaching of French classicism seems to have assumed the moralism of the Enlightenment.

This moralism went well with the characteristic which most strongly dominated classicism, the influence of ancient rhetoric. This involved a relationship not only to Cicero but also to Chrysostom and Augustine. And even though the great preachers of the early church consciously sought to free the sermon from the purely secular pattern of oratory, French classicism contributed toward restoring its lordship. Wherever its influence has penetrated, preachers have become rhetoricians. The formal renewal which it introduced in various countries has thus aided in obscuring the essential task of preaching.

More recent Catholic preaching has been almost entirely outside of the purview of the most recent historical research on preaching. No homiletical impulses of universal significance have emanated from the Roman church since the days of the great

French preachers. A tremendous area which we should consider in this study is left as a *terra incognita*. Only a few basic traits are discernible. The pure homily, which became more and more rare during the eighteenth century, appears again during the latter part of the nineteenth. A group of conscientious biblical preachers appeared within the German episcopacy, but in general, despite significant mutual influences between Catholic and Evangelical homiletics, Catholic preaching has preserved its own individuality. It is missionary and pedagogical rather than devotional. This is due to the fact that preaching generally was placed outside of the context of the mass and to a great extent assigned to specialists, missionaries and Lenten preachers from the orders who had specifically cultivated the art of spiritual oratory. Here the Jesuits more and more surpassed the other orders. Most recently we detect a growing interest in the homiletical task. This interest has left its imprint on a growing body of literature which should not be outside of the purview of evangelical theology. Scarcely anywhere in recent times have homiletical collections appeared which have been equal in breadth and depth to those which have been published in the Roman church. Here again we detect a continuity with earlier eras. A work like that of the Jesuit, Anton Koch's *Homiletisches Handbuch* published in six copious volumes in 1941, reminds us again of Bromyard's *Summa Praedicantium* and other medieval productions.

The Swiss Reformation

In church history the word Reformed has become a comprehensive name for an immeasurable variety. We may ask ourselves what unites the strict, dogmatic Presbyterian of seventeenth-century Scotland with the various forms of a Congregationalism which is basically ruleless and unfettered by all external norms. If we wish to isolate the common characteristics we will find them in the cult and in the type of worship rather than in doctrine. In cult and worship, however, there is reflected an innate tendency toward schism, toward further differentiation, and toward more and more unfettered individualism in those denominations which have abandoned the legalistic and biblically oriented soil of Presbyterianism, out of which they have all, nevertheless, emerged.

The homiletical history of the total Reformed world is still unwritten. The extensiveness of the task has been indicated by the work of a number of scholars, notably M. Schian, but thus far the absence of a guiding methodology only demonstrates the need for more thorough research. These studies have been begun in Swiss Protestantism, but Anglo-American, free church attempts at writing a history of preaching have generally been characterized by a basic individualism. A critically oriented treatment is made more difficult because the absence of method in every technical preaching pattern is itself one of the few methodical principles which is always found in Reformed preaching. Such an investigation will also receive very little guidance from the history of the various denominations because it is in the domain of preaching that the boundaries between the various denominations cease to be significant. At the same time, these very evident difficulties in this area of research make it especially appealing, for this history also includes some of the genuine high points in the history of Christian preaching.

Even in the first representatives of Reformed preaching we meet distinctive characteristics which have been preserved through the centuries. When Huldreich Zwingli (1484-1531) first began preaching in Einsiedeln in the year 1516 he spoke, in accordance with the medieval tradition, on the Gospel lessons prescribed in the mass. When he, as canon in the diocesan cathedral in Zurich, developed his own type of preaching, he did not use the pericopes but instead preached serially on the books of the Bible. This style, which also appears in Lutheran circles, was characteristic of the older Reformed preaching. The repudiation of the tradition of the pericope was related to the radical attitude toward the worship tradition of the Middle Ages. Zwingli's *Aktion oder Bruch des Nachtmahls* ("Action or Use of the Lord's Supper") of 1525 made a clean break with the tradition of the mass and created a communion service designed to be used as a congregational celebration of fellowship around the Table of the Lord.[2] This original liturgical creation left no place for preaching. It was, however, designed to be used not more than once each quarter. The Sunday service was again given a new form with the sermon as the central point. The sermon itself, loosed from its liturgical context, became the basic motif in the creation of new liturgy. It was introduced by a *votum* and the Lord's Prayer and was followed by a confession of sin, absolution, prayer and a benediction. Here Zwingli's order has, on the whole, been definitive for the development in all of Reformed Christendom. The abolition of the church year goes hand in hand with the dismemberment of the ancient liturgical context. This radical re-orientation of the place of preaching in the service created a deep and abiding distinction between Reformed and Lutheran preaching. This is not the only area where the chasm between Wittenberg and Zurich— or Geneva—seems to be deeper than the one which separates Wittenberg from Rome. The Lutheran Church has for its part sometimes emphasized faithfulness to the pericopes more than any other group in Christendom. As a result, peculiarly enough, common interests are by no means absent in Reformed and Roman preaching.

When the liturgical element is given less emphasis, it becomes necessary to give the other two basic elements, the exegetical and the prophetic, increased significance. To a cer-

---

[2] Cf. Yngve Brilioth, *Eucharistic Faith and Practice: Evangelical and Catholic,* trans. A. G. Hebert (London: SPCK, 1931).

tain degree this is also true of Zwingli's preaching. Above everything else he wished to expound the word of God and he chose two ancient homiletic masters as his models, Chrysostom and Augustine. The word was also basic for the criticism of all unbiblical churchly customs. Zwingli is hardly to be considered as prophetically inspired since for him preaching was primarily a tool to be used in the churchly and national struggle in which he was involved.

Our direct knowledge of Zwingli's preaching is meager. Only a few of his sermons have been preserved, and the treatises which are based on his oral lectures have been robbed of the form which is of interest to us in our observations. Zwingli was basically a humanist both in his criticism of the church and in his theology. The Swiss and the French Reformations participated more directly in the heritage of religious humanism than did the Lutheran. As a result of this Reformed preaching distinguished itself more than did the Lutheran by a formal culture, which is certainly only to a very small degree apparent in the heavy Swiss-German used by the Reformer from Zurich, but which from the very beginning gave Reformed preaching in the French language a special distinction, a formal elegance, which to a considerable degree was lacking in Lutheran postils.

Prophesying—*die Prophezei*—was a peculiar form of worship service in the Swiss Reformation and it became the occasion for similar gatherings in English Puritanism. These meetings were by no means designed to give opportunity for any "prophesying" in the original Christian sense. In Zurich, *die Prophezei* rather became a type of exegetical Bible study gathering for preachers and theological students. Subsequently one of the preachers delivered a devotional lecture in the church using the conversation from the gathering as the basis of his address. Several of Zwingli's commentaries as well as a part of the Zurich translation of the Bible appeared as a result of the labors of these corporate groups.

The Reformed sermon reached its classic pattern in John Calvin (1509-1564).[3] He does not compare with Luther as a popular speaker, but his sober, objective, sometimes rather dry sermons influenced Reformed Christendom more than Luther's preaching influenced Lutheranism. Calvin already had preached on certain occasions when he lived in France, but we have only scattered references to his early activity as a preacher in Geneva. He held an appointment as professor of theology from the very beginning and it was with some hesitation that he accepted as an additional responsibility the task of preaching. During his exile he served as preacher for a French refugee congregation in Strasbourg. Upon his return to Geneva he spoke regularly from the pulpit of the church of St. Pierre, usually twice every Sunday and very often on week days. We are informed that in his preaching during the decade of 1540 he intervened concretely in matters of controversy and relentlessly rebuked sin. He is reported as once having said that a hundred people from the St. Gervais section of the city were worse than animals. We very naturally draw the conclusion that during this period his preaching was supported by a strong prophetic consciousness of vocation which sometimes, with relentless power, burst into full flame. The picture which we receive from his extant sermons is, however, a wholly different one. A French refugee was appointed as preaching stenographer in Geneva in the year 1549, and as a result of his care and concern no less than approximately two thousand of Calvin's sermons from the subsequent decade are extant. On Sundays Calvin preached on the New Testament; during the week he considered the books of the Old Testament. In this way Calvin had time to go through large sections of the Bible.

[3] For further information on Calvin's preaching, consult A. Watier, *Calvin prédicateur* (1889), and especially the careful, scholarly monograph by E. Mülhaupt, *Die Predigt Calvins* ("Arbeiten zur Kirchengeschichte," Vol. XVIII, 1931).

Just as Zwingli, so Calvin also repudiated the use of the pericopes. The consideration of the church year did, nevertheless, not wholly disappear. In any case, we do possess some Easter and Pentecost sermons. In keeping with a command of the council, it was required that the history of the passion be considered during Holy Week, but this was only a survival of a custom which was due to be written off. Calvin's sermons are basically just as non-liturgical as Zwingli's. On regular Sundays the sermon was certainly the central point in a liturgical order, but this liturgical order merely served as its framework. When the Lord's Supper was celebrated according to the order of *La Forme des prieres ecclesiastiques* ("The Form of Church Prayer") the sermon might contain a reference to this celebration—at least there was to be a reminder when the next celebration would take place. Calvin's attitude on this point became very significant because of the normative position Geneva soon assumed in the family of the Reformed communions.

Accordingly, for him and for his followers preaching was a service of the word in a more exclusive sense than it was for the Lutheran preacher. The custom of using continuous biblical lections did not, however, denote a slavish confinement. Thus, Calvin sometimes did not use the individual Gospels but substituted a harmony. Sermons on the Psalms often used the rhyming paraphrases of Clément Marot (1497-1544) as a basis, and Calvin also was capable of making significant exclusions in the books of the Old Testament. The whole body of the main sections of the Bible, the law, the prophets, and the Gospels were commonly used. Even though the Gospels gained a distinct advantage by their use on Sundays, the Reformed sermon, nevertheless, to a noticeable degree became Old Testament oriented, and Reformed preaching has retained this stance throughout subsequent eras. In Calvin and his followers the exegetical interest was also an inheritance from the humanistic biblical theology which had given them their original theological impetus. Calvin the humanist has also left us a commentary on Seneca. Calvin must be awarded one of the most significant places among biblical expositors in any history of preaching. His scriptural interpretation is enriched by the fact that he more than any of his contemporaries freed himself from the traditional exegesis and especially from the affliction of allegorizing.[4] As a preacher he strove honestly to be faithful to his text, and he used his theological learning not to conceal, but rather to reveal the actual meaning of the word of Scripture. Here a fortunate storehouse of illuminating illustrations and a not mean gift of popular expression was helpful to him.

Exposition which did not apply the Scripture was, in Calvin's judgment, dead. Here the exegete becomes essentially the prophet. Some of the majesty of the word of Scripture must also envelop its proclaimers. The Savior wills that the preacher shall be "as a trumpet to gather unto himself and into his obedience the people who are his."[5] God himself is present in the preaching of the word, the God who is worthy of awe and reverence, who has elected some to salvation, others to damnation. It is in relation to the preached word that the decree of predestination becomes apparent. Calvin was by no means a stranger to the duty both of accommodating his presentation to the ability of his hearers to comprehend, and of seeking those hearers in their concrete situation. His preaching was prophetic both in interpreting God's dealings and as a significant influence in the history of the time both inside and outside of Geneva. Nothing, however, was more foreign to him than to give moralizing exhortation or pedagogical guidance in practical matters. He stood in the pulpit in order to proclaim the word of God without knowing those for whom it meant salvation or

[4] Cf. A. Jülicher, *Die Gleichnisreden Jesu*, pp. 257 ff., "Among the four main characters of the Reformation only Calvin is a truly great exegete."

[5] E. Mülhaupt, *op cit.*, p. 25.

those for whom it meant judgment. He attained a high mastery in the homiletical art of interpreting a text, whether a passage from the Gospels or a narrative from the Old Testament, without nearsighted slavishness to the order of the verses, and with an analysis of its content so profound that it became a divine message for the people who sat under his pulpit. Calvin is one of the church's greatest teachers of the art of preaching.

More Recent French Reformed Preaching

To certain greatly varying degrees the legacy of Calvin is common to all of the Reformed lines of development. Present-day American Congregationalists seem to have very little in common with the severe and cold exegete of St. Pierre. An emancipation from all liturgical fetters is, however, a common family trait, as is also an essential attachment to the word of the Bible, an attachment which has gradually become less firm. The life of this family, furthermore, has been marked by a conscious glorification of the "prophetic office," a glorification which has sometimes lapsed into an uncontrollable individualism. Linguistic and national peculiarities contend with confessional, theological and ecclesiastical-political differences. The most variegated and bewildering diversity arises out of this context. To discover and clarify distinctive boundaries and common characteristics would be an appealing assignment for our research in the history of preaching. But at this point we can only very briefly describe main streams and remind ourselves of the names which have significance for the church universal.

The most direct and elevated line extends from Calvin through the whole history of French-speaking Protestantism. The development rises to its greatest heights in the Huguenot preaching which had been refined and purified by persecution. Such Reformed preachers as Jean Claude (1619-1687) and Pierre du

157

Bosc (1623-1692) had assimilated the brilliant culture which was characteristic of the Catholic rhetoric of the era before they were exiled under the terms of the Edict of Nantes (1598). Reformed preaching experienced its greatest flowering in the exiled French congregations.

No contemporary preacher attained a higher degree of elegance in language and clarity of thought than did Jacques Saurin (1677-1730), who labored in The Hague during the last twenty-five years of his life. The extant collection of his sermons, ten volumes, is one of the truly great monuments in the history of spiritual oratory. Even though his sermons were expanded until they became dissertations which no contemporary congregation would be able to endure, the printed text preserves most of the lift and brilliance of the spoken word, especially in the effective and energetically appealing conclusions. He strove for clarity but did not turn away from the deeps. Contemporary theology might well learn something from the sermons "Concerning the Deeply Divine" and "Concerning the Beatific Vision of God." In Saurin, however, the Calvinistic proclamation experienced a thorough transformation both in content and form. For him, the orthodox Calvinistic formulations had lost their meaning. He was less the disciple of Calvin than the creator of the modern Reformed sermon. Peculiarly enough, he did not ignore the church year as completely as had his predecessors. One volume of the collection of his sermons contains festival sermons. He wished to be faithful to Scripture, but he replaced the old expository homily by a sharply logical and cogently argued address in which the short text, often a single verse of Scripture, was subservient to the subject. Most of the later Reformed preaching shows a free choice of subject, since the sermon had finally been freed from its dominance by the pericope and the rigidly exegetical tradition. The sermon exhibits genuine prophetic characteristics to the degree that it uses this freedom to illuminate actual problems and to penetrate the world of the soul with the searchlight of the gospel. Such characteristics are found in Saurin. He was anxious to preach conversion, as in the great triology "Concerning the Postponement of Conversion." In a famous digression on Louis XIV, that scourge of God, he prayed God to take the veil from the eyes of the tyrant and to forget the streams of blood which he had shed. But in other respects his addresses were dominated by a certain logical coldness and by a rational kind of argumentation which was a portent of the Enlightenment. Sometimes the sermon became an edifying moralistic essay which reminds us of Saurin's great contemporary, Tillotson. In this respect, too, Saurin anticipated the development of later Reformed preaching.

French Protestantism's homiletical tradition has continued to live through the centuries. During the nineteenth century it was fructified by the religious development in Switzerland. Alexander Vinet (1797-1847), theologian, church politician, and orator, gave final shape to his thoughts in conscious opposition to the Swiss revival. As a result of insights left by German theologians, he set the pattern for later French Protestantism's understanding of preaching; this he accomplished through his homiletics, *Homilétique ou théorie de la prédication* (published posthumously in 1853) which won readers in various countries.[6] His own preaching is naturally included in the development which emanates from Saurin. The tremendous impression which he made by his spiritual addresses was, to be sure, a result of

---

[6] [This volume appeared in English translation in 1853 under the title *Homiletics* (Edinburgh and New York). Often republished, it was long a textbook in theological seminaries in the United States. Another important volume on homiletics by Vinet was published in 1860, also posthumously, under the title *Histoire de la prédication parmi les réformés de France au dix-septième siècle* ("History of Preaching among the Reformed in France in the Seventeenth Century"). Concerning Vinet, consult the detailed article by Arnold Rüegg in *The New Schaff-Herzog Encyclopedia of Religious Knowledge* (Grand Rapids: Baker, 1953); XII, 187 ff.—TRANSLATOR.]

clarity of thought and beauty of form, but primarily it was the result of the speaker's zeal in presenting a message which was completely united with his being and deeds. He was hardly a biblical theologian. His definition of the sermon as "an address inserted in the public service" leaves no room for any extended consideration of the liturgical context.

Adolphe Monod (1802-1856), Vinet's contemporary, had, as a result of influence from the revivals in Switzerland and Scotland, been led to a spiritual intensification which made him the greatest preacher in Reformed France during the nineteenth century. He also was dependent on the legacy from the classical rhetoricians, but his sermons are permeated by biblical thought in a different way than we can find in Vinet. As a true reformed biblicist he made the various parts of the Bible equal and preferred the Old Testament and Paul to the Synoptic Gospels. The revival had led him from neological rationalism to a new appreciation of orthodox Calvinism. He also elicited arguments from the doctrine of predestination in his attempt to bring men to a decision. In his pietistic preaching the prophetic element assumes the form of a penetrating personal care of souls with an untiring zeal for making the message of sins and grace into a personally appropriated reality. This type of preaching has had few nobler representatives than Adolphe Monod.

Among those who, in our own time, have made French preaching known outside of the country is one who also bears the same name: Wilfred Monod (1867-1942). As one of the pioneers of the ecumenical movement, he served for many years, as did his namesake, as preacher at the Oratoire du Louvre in Paris. Social passion and Christian spiritualism are blended into a pattern of noble beauty in his flaming proclamation. Even though homiletics cannot simply accept the ideal of the most recent French preaching, it cannot afford to neglect the impulses to be found here.

The Puritan Tradition

Geneva was the place of origin for a whole family of churches. Influences from Calvin have left their marks on the order of worship and preaching in many lands and many parts of the world. To unravel the threads through which these influences have expressed themselves in German, Dutch, and English preaching is a tremendous task which is yet to be completed. In the case of Germany we must reckon with a constant interaction between the Lutheran and Reformed traditions, and especially with the influence that emanated from Bucer's Strasbourg, a third line of development in the history of the Reformation.

For several centuries Holland was a refuge for exiles, among whom were to be found such preachers as Thomas Cartwright (1535-1603), the father of Puritanism, and Jacques Saurin (1677-1730), the greatest Huguenot orator. The homiletical development in Holland, otherwise very little known, has not escaped being influenced by these exiles. The scarcity of preachers during the time of the Reformation led to the establishment of "schools for prophets" for the laymen, and to the founding of the University of Leyden. This is not the only instance where the demand for preaching has become a powerful stimulus in the development of higher education. Andreas Hyperius (1511-1564), the most influential homiletical theoretician of the later German Reformation, came from Ypres. His work is symbolical of the interaction between the Reformed Lutheran traditions, an interaction which no confessional struggles could stem; it is also typical of the strongly humanistic orientation of Reformed theology. During the seventeenth century, Dutch preaching became explicitly exegetical but it also bore the marks of the dogmatic struggles of the century.

The Calvinistic tradition flowered most fully in the English-speaking world. Here a tremendous field with an unsurveyable variety of personalities and an immense homiletical literature presents itself. Studies in the history of the English Reformed sermon are plentiful, but these have deliberately set their sights upon the individual preachers and on the lessons which contemporary preachers can learn from their work.

Puritanism stands in the foreground and the development is then continued in later Scotch and English Presbyterianism. Theological learning is highly treasured in these traditions and preaching has retained a certain ancient gravity for a longer time in this milieu than in other Reformed denominations. Anglicanism represents a special development in the history of preaching, even though it has many points of contact with Presbyterianism during the sixteenth and seventeen centuries. When the Puritans were forced out of the English church pulpits, they organized their own congregations as "prophesyings." This seems to designate the gathering itself rather than free preaching. The two basic characteristics in the Calvinistic tradition of preaching, the exegetical and the prophetic, appeared with monumental clarity in John Knox (c. 1505-1572). To the homiletical exposition he usually added an application in which his flaming enthusiasm for the pure gospel and his rage against idolatry were given violent personal and contemporary expression. During the subsequent centuries, the painstaking interpretation of the text more and more extinguished the spirit of prophecy, until the evangelical revival, which became the occasion for the establishment of the Scottish Free Church in the year 1843, awakening to life a new concern to reach souls with the word of life. This concern characterized the unique, formal and unwieldly preaching of Thomas Chalmers (1780-1847). During the nineteenth century both the state and the free churches produced a significant number of outstanding spiritual orators. At present the influence of the easier American style of preaching has replaced Presbyterian thoroughness.

The political and spiritual revolution which shook England during the seventeenth century acted, from the standpoint of church history, as a prism through which the disparate elements in the Puritan tradition were sundered into a variety of churchly and sectarian establishments, all the way from conservative Presbyterianism to the Quakers and the apocalyptic sects. Besides the Presbyterians, enduring significance was gained by the Independents, who later were called Congregationalists, Baptists, and Quakers. For the latter, silence at the service was more important than speaking. In a history of preaching it may be hazardous to set boundaries between the various free church developments. A study of the spiritual history of the seventeenth century in England with special reference to preaching would be a fascinating task. It could, however, not be completed without a laborious primary investigation which could not be made except in England. It is certain that the spoken word was an influence with primary significance and that preachers were sustained by a strong prophetic consciousness. It was an Anglican, Jeremy Taylor (1613-1667) who gave the widest circulation to the watchword, "liberty of prophesying," [7] but that watchword includes both the content and the final result of the whole religious struggle. The greatest name among the Presbyterians—and Anglicanism's greatest loss, even in the history of preaching—is Richard Baxter (1615-1691), who through his treatise of 1656, *The Reformed Pastor*, influenced the free church clergy for centuries, even as his meditations on *The Saints' Everlasting Rest* (1650) became one of the classic devotional books in English literature.[8] However, it is now difficult to present a picture of the character of Baxter's oral preaching. John Bunyan (1628-1688), Independent rather than Baptist, is somewhat easier to comprehend and we do have beautiful examples of his

[7] [This watchword was the title of Taylor's plea for religious liberty published in 1647.—TRANSLATOR.]

[8] Hugh Martin (ed.), *The Reformed Pastor* (Naperville, Ill.: Allenson, 1956); *The Saints' Everlasting Rest* (Westwood, N. J.: Revell, 1962).

simple soul-winning sermons. It is, however, as an author that he has made his greatest contribution to the history of preaching. It is possible to place *Pilgrim's Progress* in the context of a literary pattern which leads back to the visionary poems and biblical allegories of the Middle Ages. We may also place it in the context of the collections of homiletical illustrations from the thirteenth and fourteenth centuries. It is remarkable that the allegorical method, used so often to conceal the literal meaning of the word of the Bible, is here given the task of illuminating the Christian way of salvation. The freely constructed fable becomes an allegory. Both the imaginative character and ideational content of the book have become a gold mine for later preachers in all denominations. The book is a blending of prophecy and the care of souls which includes the most essential and the most living elements in the spiritual message of English Nonconformism. These elements make *Pilgrim's Progress* a ferment in the whole history of evangelical Christianity.

England's homiletical history during the first half of the eighteenth century leaves the observer with the impression of a flat landscape. This impression is strengthened by the fact that the name of an Anglican, John Tillotson, is the greatest name.[9] Methodist preaching does, however, rise like a tremendous mountain range above the lowlands. In modern times the spoken word has hardly ever evoked such an evident response. The personal address of the preacher has seldom reached larger groups. In a summary survey it is not possible to treat fairly the work of

[9] [It is necessary to point out that Tillotson, who was Archbishop of Canterbury and an advocate of the policy of comprehension for Nonconformists, was in fact a child of the seventeenth century. He was born in 1630 and died in 1694. It may, however, be said with confidence that he was a famous preacher on whom many divines of the eighteenth century patterned their work. Cf. James Moffatt (ed.), *The Golden Book of Tillotson* (Garden City, N. Y.: Doubleday, Doran Co., 1926).— TRANSLATOR.]

John Wesley (1703-1791) and George Whitefield (1714-1770). Here we can only make some observations.

Throughout their whole lives the founders of Methodism labored as pastors in the Church of England. Their message, however, related itself more to the Nonconformist preaching of the seventeenth century than it did to the Anglicanism of the eighteenth. In the pattern of their preaching we can perhaps find traces of the tradition of the church of their fathers. Circumstances drove them out of the church; once Wesley was denied access to his father's pulpit and instead he spoke from his father's grave in the churchyard. Whitefield became the greatest open-air preacher of all time. The descriptions of the masses who hung upon his words are almost legendary in nature. He is said to have spoken to a crowd of thirty thousand people outside Bristol. On another occasion, he himself gives the number of listeners as fifty thousand. Benjamin Franklin relates that he once walked about at a mass meeting in America where Whitefield was preaching in order to assess the carrying power of the silver-toned voice. Franklin calculated that Whitefield could actually make himself heard by thirty thousand. Not even Franklin's severe intellect, shaped by the Enlightenment, could withstand the power of the great revivalist's appealing oratory; he had originally intended to give a few pennies in the collection, but finally was impelled to give his gold and further to request a loan from his neighbors. A melodic tone of voice and an expressive shading of address were Whitefield's greatest assets. According to a well-known anecdote, Garrick the actor envied him his power of awakening the emotions of his audience merely by the way he pronounced "Mesopotamia." Whitefield's deep emotional life, which expressed itself in tears and strange gestures, worked infectiously. The "enthusiasm" which was the object of the Anglican latitudinarians' hatred left its stamp on his platform appearance. Even though Wesley's temperament and preaching style did not employ the same capacity for mass hypnosis, he also as an open-air preacher was able to gather and to captivate the masses.

Only a small portion of the strong tide of stirring words which emanated from the Methodist rostrums has been preserved. John Wesley, who sometimes spoke as often as four times on the same day and often fifteen times during the week, delivered a tremendous number of sermons even though the number forty thousand sometimes mentioned is probably myth. The sermons which were published during his lifetime have gained canonical status in Methodism.[10] Various items have been added since that time and his collected works include one hundred forty-one sermons which fill three volumes. Whitefield is said to have delivered eighteen thousand sermons, of which only sixty-five have been published. In both instances, we are hardly able to conceive the power of the spoken word from the printed sermons.

This is true of Whitefield to an even greater degree than of Wesley. Although both of them usually spoke without written notes, Wesley was, nevertheless, the man with the pen and the ordered thoughts, while Whitefield above all possessed the gift of the inspired address. Even though posterity may not be able to recover the secret of their preaching, a more careful analysis of the extant sources and the testimony of the hearers would be desirable. Wesley has become a factor of the greatest importance in the history of homiletics—through his printed sermons; indeed, memorizing some of his "standard sermons" was probably often included as part of the Methodist pastoral candidates' training. We may very well also have the right to speak of the emergence of a living type of revival sermon which arose as a result of Whitefield's influence. In any case this type of preaching has always to an essential degree found its basic pattern in Meth-

[10] There is some doubt as to whether the term "standard sermons" includes only the forty-four sermons originally published or includes nine added later. See *Wesley's Standard Sermons,* 3rd Edition, ed. E. H. Sugden (Naperville, Ill.: Allenson, 1955-56).

odism. The direct church historical influence, which Whitefield exerted on the Calvinistically oriented Anglican low church movement, was only to a very meager extent accompanied by the gift of inspired preaching.

It was very natural for the Wesley brothers and their followers not to take into consideration the liturgical context in which the sermon should be set. With this observation we surely have not solved the whole question of the relation of the sermon and the liturgy in Methodism. The cultic tradition which was take over from the Anglicanism which continued to characterize Wesley's spiritual heritage, could not have entirely escaped influencing the preacher. The Methodist sermon is not exegetical in the same sense as the older Reformed preaching. Both Whitefield and Wesley usually based their sermons on a short, freely chosen word of Scripture and this method subsequently became normal in all sermons in the English language. A series of more purely homiletical addresses is, however, extant on the Sermon on the Mount. In Wesley the exposition of the text was often given a thematic character coupled with a carefully constructed logical division. Such a division is not absent in the extant sources from Whitefield; his famous sermon on "Repentance" has four points:

"I shall, I. Show what the nature of repentance is; II. Consider the several parts and causes of repentance; III. Give you some reasons why repentance is necessary to salvations; and, IV. Exhort all of you, high and low, rich and poor, one with another, to endeavor after repentance." [11]

All Methodist preaching is saturated with an attempt to make the central biblical message, as it was understood, living. Just as it was once true in the case of Luther, so now also there appeared a radical concentration on reconciliation, on sin and grace. In Wesley this central motif was united with a zeal for

[11] C. E. Macartney (ed.), *Great Sermons of the World* (Boston: Stratford, 1926), p. 214.

sanctification which left its imprint on Methodist ethics; in Whitefield the emphasis on sanctification was united with the doctrine of election and this gave his call to repentance its penetrating power.

The prophetic characteristic does, however, appear most powerfully throughout the whole movement. It emerges as the consciousness of a special call to preach the gospel to the poor and disinherited. Methodism's pure proclamation of the gospel became a tremendous social and political force. It was the address to the individual which was the basic emphasis in those popular preachers. The individualizing of the sermon, its "thou" character, appeared in bold contrast to the discreet exhortations of the conventional sermon. This stance has now become obsolete because of irritating misuse, but when the personally aggressive tone of the mission proclamation, directed at those who were within the church, was new and fresh, it must have exhibited tremendous power. Nearly all of the more recent revival preachers have copied the ideas and modes of expression which were characteristic of the first Methodists.[12]

The whole history of English Nonconformism during the nineteenth century is reflected in a rising tide of homiletical literature. Here again a detailed study would offer much that is of interest. One man's contribution, above all others, has attained universal significance. Charles Haddon Spurgeon (1834-1892) surely can bear comparison with the fathers of Methodism if we consider the range and size of the crowds which gathered

---

[12] The following quotation from Wesley is illuminating in this context: "Dost thou hear the Saviour calling *to thee* to repent and turn? Was it not for thee that he shed his blood? Did he not carry thy sorrows to Calvary, even thine? Was he not wounded for thy transgressions? Did he not think of thee, of thy soul and of all its abominations, that dark night when he lay in agony on the ground? Yes. It was none other than thy sins that made him sweat blood in that garden. But now with a purpose of mercy in his heart toward thy wretched soul, he calls thee to himself; and says, yes, he says it to thee, 'Come now let us reason together.'" Quotation from C. Smyth, *The Art of Preaching* (London: SPCK, 1953), p. 171.

to hear him. For him, every meeting place became too small. The Metropolitan Tabernacle, which was built especially for his use, had six thousand seats and the seats were filled Sunday after Sunday for thirty years. Spurgeon extemporized, often using only a few lines in a notebook, but the sermons were taken down in shorthand and published after they had been edited by the speaker. Fifteen volumes of the magazine "The Metropolitan Tabernacle" were filled in this way. Individual sermons were published in enormous editions and translated into several languages. In some years the German market sold twenty-one thousand copies. Spurgeon tops all records both in respect to publicity and range of extant production. In this unique production from this spiritually alive Baptist, who left a Congregationalist congregation and who finally came into conflict with the Baptist denomination (which he considered as having deserted true orthodoxy), the spirit of the old Puritanism breaks out in full flower for the last time—in the era of industrialism and capitalism. Spurgeon set his stamp upon free church preaching for at least a generation through his example, his efforts in the training of pastors, as well as through a series of books which were intended as helps for the preacher.[13]

A nonliturgical character has hardly ever appeared to such a marked degree as it did in Spurgeon's tabernacle, which was not designed to be anything but a meeting place to house an audience. To a greater degree than many of his contemporaries and predecessors Spurgeon wished to be an exegete. With his whole soul he held fast to an uncompromising doctrine of inspiration and in dependence upon the Reformed and especially the Puritan tradition he selected his texts and subjects just as readily from the Old Testament as from the New. In common with the first Methodists, he captivated the crowd by speaking to the individual, very often in a conversational tone, concern-

---

[13] [Cf. Helmut Thielicke, *Encounter with Spurgeon* (Philadelphia: Fortress Press, 1963).—TRANSLATOR.]

ing the seriousness of sin and the riches of grace. The fact that he limited himself to the Pauline gospel, a trait which he shared with all of the older Nonconformists, was counterbalanced by his ability successfully to individualize and, more especially, by his skillful use of illustrations, the *exempla* of the Middle Ages in modern dress. Spurgeon can surely claim a place in the procession of evangelical prophetic preachers. He did, however, prophesy for the individual and not for the community. He was not the herald of a new era; rather, we may say, that a great era was buried together with him.

The last generation of free church preachers, like their contemporaries in other denominations, bear in many respects the imprint of a time of spiritual crisis. They are not cast in the same mold as the old Puritans. The dogmatic differences have lost most of their relevance. Improved theological training has undermined the doctrine of inspiration, the bedrock, which gave Spurgeon his unshakable stability. A new openness to the voices of the age, a wider choice of subjects, and a conscious psychological training cannot, however, substitute for the old concern for saving souls through the proclamation of the word. Many personalities deserve closer study, especially W. H. Selbie (born 1862) who in his many years of service at Mansfield College in Oxford made a great contribution in training the younger generation of free church preachers.

American Preaching

The confrontation of the British and American traditions, each with the other, is a decisive influence in the most recent Nonconformist and Presbyterian preaching. Its world-inclusive character makes the Anglo-Saxon free church movement of today especially significant. Even though the smaller limbs in the British imperial organism have made their contributions, the

United States must, however, be placed in the foreground. In the area of preaching the New World was certainly for a long time dependent on its relations to the Old, but North American Protestantism soon assumed its own face. This happened during the eighteenth century when the Congregationalist Jonathan Edwards (1703-1758) by his harrowing proclamation of the basic tenet of Calvinism, the sovereignty of God, called forth the first of the great revivals which placed their stamp upon the spiritual history of the United States. His best known sermon, "Sinners in the Hands of an Angry God," describes with dreadful clarity how God consigns sinners to the fires of hell. Through his book, *The Freedom of the Will* (1754) Edwards attained a place among the foremost theologians in American history. Edwards' successor as president of Princeton University, the Presbyterian Samuel Davies (1724-1761), must also be included among the great preachers.

The nineteenth century presents a rich and varied picture. The multiplicity of denominations, on the one hand, with an almost endless variety of spiritual types and most varied educational standards in the congregations and among the preachers, and the highly developed cult of the spoken word in a young democratic community on the other hand, join in making the most recent homiletical history of American Christendom into an impenetrable forest to the outsider. Individual sermons have won special renown, such as Eliphalet Nott's (1773-1866) sermon on "The Sin of Duelling" (1804). A few personalities very obviously rise above the crowd. The Presbyterian, Lyman Beecher (1775-1863) exerted a tremendous influence both by his example and by his work as a teacher. His name has been given to a well known lectureship on homiletics at Yale University which has very significantly stimulated an interest in the practical and theoretical problems of preaching. His son Henry Ward Beecher (1813-1887), outshone him by far as a popular orator and his extemporaneous, often dramatically constructed sermons, illustrate the character of American preaching in both its weaknesses and strength. The Unitarian sermon, whose chief exponents were William Ellery Channing (1780-1842) and Theodore Parker (1810-1860), is a unique contribution to American preaching. Its liberal interpretation of Christianity also became an influence in the spiritual history of other countries. Greater influence—and from a different point on the theological spectrum—was exerted by Charles Grandison Finney (1792-1875) and Dwight L. Moody (1837-1899); the voice of the latter has perhaps reached farther than any other American preacher. Although Bishop Phillips Brooks (1835-1893) strictly speaking belongs in another context as an Anglican, he must be included here since preaching in the Episcopal Church in America does not constitute a sharply defined area. Brooks must assume a position next to Henry Ward Beecher from the standpoint of fame. His preaching, however, exhibits a more aristocratic orientation and, perhaps, he has meant most to posterity through his lectures on the art of preaching, entitled simply *Lectures on Preaching* (1877).

The modern American sermon is the final development in the homiletical history of Reformed Christendom. The distance from Calvin to S. Parkes Cadman (1864-1936) and Harry Emerson Fosdick (born 1878) is great; these are probably the greatest names in American preaching in most recent times. Freedom from all liturgical fetters is perhaps the most evident and the most common basic characteristic of American preaching in every era: the great Christian festivals have set their stamp upon preaching only to a very small degree and, in contrast, the national holidays have demanded special attention. Complete freedom in the choice of texts, to be sure, opens the possibility for connected series of sermons as well as the opportunity for paying attention to the situation of the times. But on the other hand the church year's invaluable corrective against personal one-sideness and a constricted choice of subjects has been lost.

The scurry for the practically edifying and the emotionally impelling easily pushes the great fact of salvation in the history of revelation into the background. Faithfulness to the Bible also suffers when the text is only a short word of Scripture which is chosen merely as a starting point for the treatment of a specific subject which has been determined earlier. The ecumenical emphasis appears much more sharply of late, leveling the boundaries between churches and confessions. At the same time, the main lines of development within American Protestantism are generally more significant than individual denominational homiletical traditions and ideals.

When the Reformed sermon ceased to be properly exegetical, it was more and more compelled to exalt the prophetic element. This appears very clearly in most of the Anglo-Saxon presentations on the task of preaching.[14] It is very evident that this implies a profound contrast to the way the Lutheran tradition understands the proclamation of the word, and it is also evident that the Lutheran tradition stands closer to the view of the sermon which appeared in the ancient church. It is clear, furthermore, that the prophetic deed when it has been detached from the other basic elements of the sermon can be understood in radically different ways. When the concern of the older Calvinism for proclaiming the counsel of the transcendent God to the children of the times has taken on an archaic character, when the revivalist's ardor for reaching sinners with his message of repentance has been cooled, "prophecy" must be given an extremely vague content. It may be placed in the service of a this-worldly zeal for world betterment or it may become a series of universal reflections on the problems of the spiritual

---

[14] A twentieth-century Presbyterian, W. P. Merrill, began the 1922 Lyman Beecher Lectures with this statement: "The prophet is the preacher's ideal. The humblest preacher looks at the spokesman of God, afire with the truth, filled with the Spirit, accredited by the touch of the Eternal Word, and says, 'that is what I would be, if I could.'" *The Freedom of the Preacher* (New York: Macmillan, 1922).

life. The otherwise commendable attempt to address the children of the age in the language of the time can become a temptation to forget the eternal, that which is true for every generation. Formal proficiency may create a literate and cultivated essay style which sells the proper language of preaching short. Other preachers can learn a great deal from the Americans both about a vital encounter with mankind over matters which concern them, and about language which bears the mark of reality. Nevertheless, a critical evaluation is necessary because of the growing influence which the American style of preaching most likely will exert in the future.

Anglicanism

In richness, the history of preaching in the Anglican church cannot be compared to the Nonconformist tradition. From the standpoint of fundamentals, however, it is of special significance. The similarities with the Reformed development are evident, but in the Anglican church a restraining influence was present: in common with Lutheran Christendom the Anglicans to some extent preserved the liturgical context of the sermon. To this we may also add the fact that hardly anywhere in Reformed Christendom has the continued influence of the medieval method of preaching been so evident and so constant as in England.

The relation between liturgy and preaching in the Anglican church is, however, a very complicated question. As long as the service of the Lord's Supper retained its character as a high mass, as was the case in the *First Prayer Book of Edward VI* (1549) it was natural for the sermon to maintain its place in the service and to be based upon the established pericopes. The collection of model sermons, *Book of Homilies,* edited by Thomas Cranmer in 1547, was based upon these pericopes and was a parallel exhibit to the Lutheran postils.[15] Its influence on the later history of preaching was meager. But when the mass became a communion service, as in the *Books of Common Prayer* of 1552 and 1559 (also 1662), the service no longer offered a natural place for a sermon directed at the whole congregation. It is, nevertheless, very probable that as a result of the high church movement during the time of Charles I who reigned from 1625 to 1649, the mass remained as the main service and also included preaching. But later developments pushed aside the communion mass and made morning and evening prayer the best-attended worship services on Sunday. No organic place for the sermon was found in these prayer offices. The sermon became a nonliturgical addition even though it was set in the framework of hymn singing, itself a later addition to the old liturgical order.

The result of all this was that the pericopes ceased to be used as preaching texts. Instead, the later Reformed custom of speaking on a short passage of Scripture, which had the character of a word of introduction or motto rather than of an actual text, was introduced. A great portion of the extant homiletical literature exhibits this character and is hardly distinguishable in any formal sense from the Reformed practice. This does not mean that the liturgical element was entirely lost. There remained the church year, to which the Anglican preachers never ceased to give their attention, and here the church year to some extent exhibited a richer fabric than in the Lutheran practice, because of the conservative retention of the old calendar of saints' days. Very often preaching texts were chosen from the pericopes or from other liturgical passages such as one of the Psalms appointed for the day. The constant use of the Psalms and some of the other liturgical elements in the prayer offices did not fail to set its stamp upon the language of preaching. The absence of

---

[15] The first *Book of Homilies* was succeeded in 1563 by a second, edited by Parker and Jewel.

an established liturgical setting for the act of preaching itself, as well as the possibility of a free choice of texts has, however, doubtless exerted a decisive influence on the development of homiletics. The Anglicans have felt the need for an established form for the sermon to a much lesser degree than the Lutherans, but, on the other hand, they have possessed the possibility of considering a variety of subjects which could not appropriately be included as an interpretation of the pericopes.

The more recent high church movement, however, has brought forth a significant change. Where high mass has again become the main Sunday service, it has usually also included a sermon. Even though compulsory pericopes have never been proposed for preaching, the connection with the church year and the special message of the day has become more fixed. Yet it would be incorrect to maintain that this has brought about any profound change in the character of preaching. The over-emphasis on the liturgy has seldom given sufficient opportunity for solid preaching; a certain undervaluation of preaching has not been unusual. The significant spiritual orators, who have arisen out of the high church movement, have very often been strongly influenced by the homiletical patterns of other Anglo-Saxon denominations. Sometimes the splendor of the mass has become a poorly styled background for a short spiritual chat. Preaching has been given a better opportunity at other occasions as at vespers or at special services which very often have had a missionary character.

The inheritance from the Middle Ages grew in influence within the church in direct proportion to the divergence between Anglicanism and Puritanism. It has been said that Anglican preaching followed the paths of the Middle Ages until late in the seventeenth century when a strong reaction against the antiquated forms developed.[16] Bishop Lancelot Andrewes (1555-

[16] Cf. Smyth, *op. cit.*, pp. 99-166.

1626), whose preaching won the admiration of the age of James I but who was wholly rejected by the critics of the eighteenth century, is the best example in showing how the medieval *artes praedicandi* deeply influenced a more recent era. Andrewes placed the *exordium* with a closing prayer ahead of the text and the beginning of the sermon proper. He excelled in a minute division of his theme, he loved Latin and Greek citations and an ingenious play on words, but at the same time he did not worship form for its own sake. He was a devout man and a serious theologian and the Spinozistic subject arrangement was usually a real expression of a thoughtful and laborious dialectic.[17] We can only regret that this technically disciplined preaching style, which is similar in many respects to the art of preaching in Lutheran orthodoxy and which was driven to excess by Andrewes and his imitators, has so completely been thrown overboard in later Anglican preaching.

Another development of the Middle Ages, the illustrative sermon, is represented by Bishop Hugh Latimer (born c. 1485 and burned at the stake in 1555) and it was completely developed by Jeremy Taylor (born in 1613 and died in 1667 as Bishop of Down and Connor in Ireland). Here we meet some of the bizarre illustrative world of *Master Physiologus* and the old collections of moralistic anecdotes. Taylor makes use of the whole of Noah's Ark: the silkworm is an illustration of the development of the soul, the bee's busy life illuminates the blessing of marriage, the crocodile who is always growing exhibits the danger of sinful habits. Taylor possessed a poetic

---

[17] The division of the subject in a purely grammatical way is peculiar to Andrewes; consequently in a sermon on the word "Immanuel" he preached on the letters in the word and extracted devotional lessons from each. T. S. Eliot, one of the most fastidious contemporary critics, paid Andrewes a high compliment: "Andrewes may seem pedantic and verbal. It is only when we have saturated ourselves in his prose, followed the movement of his thought, that we find his examination of words terminating in the ecstasy of assent." Quotation from Smyth, *op. cit.,* p. 125.

nature and was one of the great masters of English prose. His exaggerated homiletical use of figurative language did, however, contribute toward bringing it into discredit.

A new era in English preaching appeared with John Tillotson (1634-1694). In his search for a more natural style he had predecessors in Bishop John Wilkens of Chester (1614-1672) who in 1646, in the publication *Ecclesiastes or the Gift of Preaching,* had demanded a less artificial method of preaching, and Robert South (1634-1716) who with youthful boldness in 1660 in a sermon at Oxford, "The Scribe Instructed to the Kingdom of Heaven," made an attack on "metaphysical artificiality." By parentage and training Tillotson belonged to the Puritans, and his spiritual development had been influenced by the Cambridge Platonists. At the time of the Restoration he found his way unnoticed into the Anglican church where his unusual gifts as an orator together with his gentle amiability, which was characteristic both of his person and his theology, led him to the highest places of honor. He would gladly have wished to spend his whole life as the Dean of St. Paul's, but was prevailed upon to accept the Archbishop's office in Canterbury, which he occupied only for a period of three years. It is very easy to compare him to his great contemporaries in France. He did not possess, nor did he seek, their flaming rhetoric, but at the same time there was something characteristically classical in his unadorned clarity. His unique renown may be puzzling to posterity. Neither his calmly reasoned style nor his rational moralism appear to be stimulating. A well-known sermon, "The Precepts of Christianity not Grievous," exhibits many of the distinctive features of the religion of the Enlightenment. The secret of Tillotson's success may perhaps depend upon the fact that he anticipated the tastes and spiritual orientation of the coming centuries. In a purely formal sense he cleaned house, sweeping away the methods of both the older high churchliness and Puritanism. His strength lay in a clear and transparent subject arrangement, with a stated subject and detailed development, often divided into three parts, which very naturally grew out of the theme.

There may be only slight traces of the sermon's cultic context in Tillotson's literary production. He was hardly an exegete, much less a prophet. Through him "the sermon lost its heroic note and became a moral essay, the mediator of a sober, utilitarian, prudential ethic rather than a proclamation of the gospel of the Kingdom of God."[18] The essay type of sermon, which because of this pattern stands essentially outside the established homiletical form which had been developed through the centuries, became the model for Anglicanism's spiritual oratory for more than a century. Many pastors of the eighteenth century edified their rural congregations by reading aloud from Tillotson. His sermons have been translated into many languages.

The Anglican sermon to a disheartening extent became an oral essay on a religious or ethical subject. Creditable attempts to give preaching a greater spiritual depth and individual preachers of high caliber appear against this background. The most serious attempt to revive preaching came from evangelicalism. Here no person was more significant than Charles Simeon (1759-1836), who was for many years university instructor in Cambridge, fellow of King's college, and vicar of Holy Trinity. His untiring labor in training preachers took shape in a giant magazine of sermon outlines, *Horae Homileticae,*[19] in 21 volumes and containing 2,536 subject arrangements. He was, however, more influential as a result of the impulses which

---

[18] *Ibid.,* p. 160.

[19] "*Horae Homileticae*: or Discourses (principally in the form of Skeletons) now first digested into one continued series, and forming a Commentary upon every book of the Old and New Testament: to which is annexed, an improved edition of a translation of Claude's Essay on the Composition of a Sermon" (1832-33). The preface suggests that if the reader studies one outline each day, he can continue reading for a period of seven years.

he set in motion through his oral teaching than he was through his general orientation and his pedantic and forbidding *Homiletics*. He forced his students to take their homiletical responsibility with the utmost seriousness. He derived his principles of sermon construction from the work of the famous Huguenot preacher Jean Claude (1619-1687), *Treatise on the Composition of a Sermon*. Since this work stems from the classical tradition, which grew out of the *artes praedicandi* of the Middle Ages, the old tradition once again became a living influence in English preaching through the work of Simeon.

The new high churchliness which grew out of the Oxford movement is, in its earlier phases, a notable chapter in the history of Anglican preaching. This is not the only area where this more recent high churchliness has accepted the legacy of the older evangelicalism. We certainly do not encounter any counterpart of Simeon's concern for technique and training, but this is counter-balanced by the power of living example. John Henry Newman (1801-1890) won his position of spiritual leadership mainly by his preaching in the university church, St. Mary the Virgin. It is very possible that these famous sermons have been overrated. They were essays delivered orally and are preserved in this form. Here we meet not only a loving penetration of the word of Scripture but most of all an intense conviction of the reality of the world of God and a zeal for the care of souls which gives the academically constructed lecture the character of a prophetic message. Newman both before and after his conversion to Rome remains unquestionably one of the great preachers in the history of the church. None of the enormous number of other sermons from this high church movement quite attain the class of mastership. Some are, however, worthy of further study. This is especially true of the formally heavy, but religiously intense preaching of E. B. Pusey (1800-1882); in his work the church year has received renewed attention.

Neither Simeon nor Newman exerted an influence comparable to that which emanated from the unpretentious pulpit of Frederick W. Robertson (1816-1853) in Brighton.[20] Even though he did not wish to belong to any churchly party, he nevertheless represents the best in broad churchliness: the wide vision, the ethical seriousness, the rational clarity which in Robertson is deepened into a strong awareness of the dimension of infinity, the awareness of the significance of the trembling intuitions of the life of the spirit. In many respects he appears as the heir of Tillotson. His divisions are simpler and he is inferior to Tillotson in logical rigor. The calmly argumentative essay style is common to both of them. Robertson does, however, possess much greater depth. He is wholesomely textual and often gives a penetrating analysis of biblical personalities and thoughts. He has also left behind homiletical commentaries on Genesis and the Letters to the Corinthians. It is primarily his psychological sharp-sightedness, his rich and delicately shaded message to the individual, which gives his preaching its position in the classic devotional literature of Christendom.

A sketchy survey of the most recent Anglican preaching can hardly escape relating itself to the three main lines of development in England's more recent church history. It is strikingly difficult to find any really significant representatives of the evangelical tradition. Liverpool's first bishop, John Charles Ryle (1816-1900), was perhaps the best known and most highly appreciated. But if we could make an overall evaluation of the low church contribution to Sunday preaching in countless parish churches we surely would gain a totally different picture. It has been evangelicalism's historic task always to defend the sermon's right to a place in the service and its right to be considered an essential feature of the work of the pastor.

The broad church movement cannot be clearly differentiated

---

[20] Cf. *The Preaching of F. W. Robertson*, ed. Gilbert E. Doan, Jr. (Philadelphia: Fortress Press, 1964).

either from evangelicalism or from high churchliness: to an essential degree it has acted as a spiritual ferment which has to some extent also influenced the other movements. During the final years of the Victorian era, William Boyd Carpenter (1841-1918), Bishop of Ripon and later a canon of Westminster, won great renown as a spiritual orator, especially at court. He represents a synthesis of evangelical tradition and liberal thought which especially expressed itself in his popular Bible commentaries. His lectures on the art of preaching, delivered in 1895, are interesting, especially his development of the technique of delivery. The broad church tradition has significant contemporary representatives: Herbert Hensley Henson (1863-1947), who steeped his often ethical, very often polemically oriented oratory in a pattern which shows dependence upon the great speakers of French classicism, and W. R. Inge (1860-1954), in whom a mystical vein broke through the rational presentation in a very wholesome way. Inge was the foremost representative of the Platonic orientation in Christian thought in the contemporary world.

We are hardly justified in including two learned biblical scholars, the one succeeding the other as Bishop of Durham, J. B. Lightfoot (1828-1889) and B. F. Westcott (1825-1901), within the high church movement since they continued to be exegetes when they were in the pulpit. In his extensive homiletical production Westcott also emerged as a significant theological scholar. For him as well as for the preachers who had come out of the tradition of the Oxford movement, the doctrine of the incarnation was the basic theme. The great name in the generation following Newman and Pusey, from the standpoint of the high church movement, was Henry Parry Liddon (1829-1890), a significant biblical preacher who with real intensity could draw a message out of the Old Testament and address it to the contemporary world. Since his time, exegetical preaching has had very few outstanding representatives.[21]

When liberal thought, especially its historic understanding of the Bible, was united with the high church tradition in Bishop Gore (1853-1932) and his school, preaching gained a wider perspective and a new stimulus. Here the theology of the incarnation became the bridge from academic thought to an intense social interest which in H. Scott Holland's (1847-1918) altogether too wordy, but uncommonly captivating preaching acquired a great deal of prophetic fire and exaltation. The Archbishop of Canterbury, William Temple (1881-1944), became his foremost disciple. Temple has hardly any competition for first place among the preachers in the Anglican church in our era. In him many traditional developments met and were melted together in a living unity, but it is primarily the social concern which in Temple and in others is able to break through the inherited essay style with a deeply personal message. Here, closely associated, we are reminded of one of Anglo-Catholicism's most inspired preachers, G. A. Studdert-Kennedy (1883-1929), a passionate and realistic popular orator, whose message has also preserved much of its fire in the printed word.

The distance between the great names and the rank and file is very great, especially in Anglo-Catholicism. In this respect the heritage from the Oxford movement has been badly administered. A certain tendency appears, perhaps as a result of conscious dependence on Roman practice, to let preaching, especially the preaching of revival and renewal, be a task for the specialists. This development has been strengthened by the Anglican orders. These, such as The Society of St. John the Evangelist (the Cowley Fathers) and The Community of the Resurrection in Mirfield, have very often supplied speakers for

[21] To be sure, we should be reminded of the exegete who died early in life, Sir Edwyn Hoskyns (1884-1937), and his *Cambride Sermons* (London: SPCK, 1938).

the evangelistic missions which have become especially characteristic of high church pastoral interests. Significant preachers have emerged out of the orders and in addition to Charles Gore, himself one of the founders of the brotherhood in Mirfield, we can name Walter H. Frere (1863-1938), Bishop of Truro until 1935. A member of the Community of the Resurrection, Paul B. Bull, has written the most complete and the most modern guide on the art of preaching which has been published in twentieth-century England.[22]

A study of Bull's instructive work shows clearly how Anglican preaching has to a high degree been influenced by the Reformed tradition. The preacher must be both prophet and priest, but never does the author consider the relation between preaching and liturgy, and the church year is hardly mentioned. This high churchly homiletics shows how completely the tradition has ceased to consider preaching a deed within the context of worship. The prophet's task is to impart three types of instruction: dogmatic, ethical and exegetical. The interpretation of the Bible, however, becomes a special type of preaching, not its perpetual nerve. In the usual sermon it is the common practice to select the subject first; the choice of a text takes place at the conclusion of the preparation. Bull draws freely from sources in secular rhetoric, and we can also detect the distant influence of the homiletical art of the Middle Ages in his thought-provoking regulations for the division and construction of the sermon. The humanistic view of the sermon as one type of oratory among others prevents him from gaining a firm understanding of the uniqueness of preaching. This is just as true of the practice of Anglican preaching as it is of its theory and is, perhaps, the primary reason for its evident weaknesses—in spite of its creditable impulses and brilliant examples.

[22] *Lectures on Preaching and Sermon Construction* (London: Macmillan, 1922).

The History of Preaching In Sweden

TRANSLATOR'S NOTE: This appendix is a summary of two chapters in the original Swedish edition of this book. As far as possible an attempt has been made to preserve the author's style and pattern of thought, but it has seemed wise to select only those portions of the two chapters which appear most relevant to the English-speaking world. Quotations have been translated directly from Archbishop Brilioth's text.

The Medieval Background

Gustavus I Vasa (1496?-1560), Sweden's first Protestant king, was most certainly exaggerating when he asserted that before the time of the Reformation preaching was not heard in the churches of Sweden more often than during "church mass." Protestants have been altogether too prone uncritically to accept this evaluation of the Middle Ages in Sweden. The fact is that during the latter part of this era the bishops often stressed the parish pastor's duty to expound the gospel in the vernacular, even though such exposition was seldom thought of as anything but an unsophisticated paraphrase. To this paraphrase the preachers added the reading of some of the main sections of the catechism, and, seeking to make the exposition of the text instructional, they sometimes also added a type of general confession which corresponded to the German *offene schuld* or the English prone.[1]

The rather extensive sources which are the basis of our knowledge of preaching in medieval Sweden have been explored only to a very limited extent. Fortunately, however, the greatest personality in this history, the Canon of Linköping, Magister Mathias (d. 1350), who was the teacher and confessor of St. Birgitta (c. 1303-1373), has been the object of careful study.[2] Mathias' extensive writings, especially his *Copia Exemplorum*, deal in large measure with preaching; they compare favorably with the era's best homiletical literature. Mathias towers above all others as the mediator of the Scholastic tradition from the University of Paris and, indeed, of the entire Dominican tradition of scholarship. Several passages in St. Birgitta's writings show that the preaching of Mathias had great influence, and with respect to preaching—as in so many other respects—the living conscience of the Middle Ages spoke through St. Birgitta.

During the fourteenth century the mendicant friars were perhaps the most significant popular preachers in Sweden. In this connection we must mention the Dominican monastary at Sigtuna. Algot of Skara, a Franciscan who lived during the time of St. Birgitta, gained recognition because "in countless sermons to the multitudes he warmed the hearts of his hearers in a wonderful way."[3]

The influence of the mendicant friars was soon dwarfed by the brothers from Vadstena. We are constantly amazed at the contribution this little group of thirteen ordained monks made toward the growth of a churchly culture, although our judgment may be influenced somewhat by the fact that sources are here available. Most of the Swedish manuscripts which we possess

[1] Cf. p. 93 above.

[2] B. Strömberg, *Magister Mathias och fransk mendikantpredikan* ("Samlingar och studier till Svenska kyrkans historia," Vol. IX; 1944).

[3] Cf. *Svenska kyrkans historia*, II, 727.

from the Middle Ages have their origin in Vadstena. In completeness of detail no other cloister chronicles can rival those from Vadstena, and our collection of medieval Swedish postils comes from this same cloister.[4] These postils, which are the first great legacy on the history of preaching in Sweden available to us in print, give a good picture of preaching at Vadstena.

We will be able to gain a more complete picture of late medieval preaching only after we have studied all of the original manuscripts available and paid special attention to their homiletical content. Almost without exception they stem from Vadstena and are now housed in the library at Uppsala University. In this connection we should note that there appeared, in 1942, a collection of medieval sermons on St. Henrik (d. 1156), the patron saint of Finland, together with a survey of contemporary sermons on the saints.[5] In this publication, sermons for major feasts of the church year are represented along with a large number of sermons for special seasons. The Bible is richly present in these sermons, which were probably preached in the vernacular, but it appears mainly as citations interspersed in the text. Passages from the church fathers were often quoted along with references to Scripture. The historic attachment to the life of the saints is very loose, and the total composition leaves the impression of a dialectic play or a pearl tapestry where thoughts, citations, and ornamental flourishes have been woven together in a geometric pattern designed to waken amazement rather than to edify. This preaching, full of ostentatious learning and vain labor, had lost its way and represented only a withdrawal from its essential task.

---

[4] Published in *Svenska Fornskriftssällskapets Samlingar,* 23:1-5 (1879, 1880, 1893, 1905-1906, 1909-1910).

[5] A. Maliniemi (ed.), *De S. Henrico episcopo et martyre: Die Mittelalterliche Literatur über den Apostel Finnlands, II* ("Finska kyrkohistoriska samfundets handlingar," 45:2; 1942).

Olaus Petri and the Renewal of Preaching

Against this background the preaching of the Reformation appears in bold relief. This is especially evident in the central place assumed by preaching in the worship and order of the reformed church. It is also apparent in the new demands which were placed upon the preacher, demands which were only to a very limited extent satisfied.

The early history of the Swedish Reformation is closely related to preaching. When Dr. Nicolaus, the Dean of Strångnås, in 1523 listed the heresies of Olaus Petri (1493-1552), he concerned himself only with those matters which the new deacon had presented in his sermons. Johannes Messenius' chronicle on Stockholm (1612) gives information concerning the new pulpit which was built for Master Olov and from which "he was driven with sticks, shoes and stones."

The only authentically reformatory sentence in the *Recess of Våsterås* (1527) is found in the fourth paragraph, ". . . and they are requested that the word of God should be preached in its purity everywhere in the kingdom." [6] This is further developed in the first section of the regulations on ordination where it is stated that if the bishops are not able to furnish the vacant districts with preachers who can preach and who wish to preach the word of God, then the king may appoint another candidate "more ready to do so." In a remarkably restrained tone the Våsterås decisions gave expression to the same thought that Olaus Petri had uttered more sharply and clearly when he

[6] [The call to the Diet of Våsterås stated, "In order that an agreement might be reached in the religious dispute which has arisen here as well as in the rest of Christendom—and if it be not peaceably settled in time it can be understood what ill effects may follow." Quoted in Conrad Bergendoff, *Olaus Petri and the Ecclesiastical Transformation in Sweden* (New York: The Macmillan Co., 1928), p. 31. The term "recess" is used to signify the common formula adopted by the estates at the Diet.—TRANSLATOR.]

said, "The preacher's office is to proclaim the word of God just as the blacksmith's office is blacksmithing."

Definite prescriptions concerning the content of the sermon and its instructional form soon appeared alongside the formal demand that sermons be preached. A still bolder and more prophetic tone is apparent in Olaus Petri's exposition of the duties of an evangelical preacher in his treatise of 1535, *Exhortation Addressed to All Evangelical Preachers.* The more stringent requirements of the state church, which characterized the ecclesiastical politics of Gustavus I Vasa in the 1530's and 1540's, prescribed another duty: Preachers must exhort the people to obey the authorities. To the degree that evangelical preaching became a significant influence on public opinion it became an object of concern to those in authority. Here it is true, as is often the case in the later Reformation period in Sweden, that the influence of Melanchthon is more apparent than that of Luther.

The annals of Swedish preaching include no greater name than Olaus Petri.[7] More than any other minister, Petri deserved the title *verbi divini minister.* His whole ministry was characterized by a solicitude for preaching. All else was subservient to that sovereign interest. He did, however, soon discover, that the "sound and tone" of the word of the gospel did not waken the same response in others as in himself and that it was necessary for preaching helps to be placed in the hands of pastors.

The Swedish New Testament of 1526 had been published so that the word of God might be read at home, in the mother tongue, as well as at the services, where the old forms and the Latin language were still used. A catalog of pericopes, the skeleton of a Swedish lectionary, was appended to the translation, probably as an aid for preachers who wished to add the

[7] [Conrad Bergendoff's study of the Swedish Reformation just referred to is the best English source.—TRANSLATOR.]

Swedish readings to the Latin lections, perhaps with a short explanation. This was a substitute for the sermon, which had probably been prevalent in the Swedish church during the Middle Ages. We cannot state with any degree of certainty who edited the catalog; possibly it was Olaus Petri himself. If he did so, it was rather as a concession to the immediate situation than out of personal conviction. His personal attitude to the pericope system is both uncertain and disputed; probably to him, as to Luther, it was an issue of minor significance. That the gospel itself be preached was primary.

"Many simple clerics" complained that they could not preach to the people with the help of the text alone. Olaus Petri prepared sermon helps for them by translating a part of "the German postil which has recently been published." His preface neglected to state, perhaps for ecclesio-political reasons, that Luther was the author of the volume. The translation included sermons from Luther's summer postil of 1526, but omitted certain parts which Petri considered not useful. The omissions included an altogether too sharp polemic against certain customs of the Roman Catholic church and a couple of ghost stories. We may also well ask why the translator arbitrarily stopped his work in the middle of the Trinity season. Perhaps he thought, with good reason, that Luther's sermon for the eighth Sunday after Trinity, the Sunday of the false prophets, would be entirely too difficult for the Swedes to digest. Petri retained the collection of Gospels which the German editors had borrowed from Bugenhagen's *Indices in evangelia dominicalia* (1524).[8] In his preface to the volume, moreover, Petri expressed very evident reservations about the whole work. The translation had been prepared hurriedly in order to give preachers an indication of how they should proceed in their interpretation of the Gospel lesson. Petri intended very soon "to have published another simple postil on the Gospels for the whole church year." More

[8] Cf. p. 120 above.

than two hundred years would elapse before Luther's church postil would become a popular book in Sweden.

In 1530, Olaus Petri redeemed his promise to publish a complete postil. The "Little Postil" arose partly as a result of the desires expressed by the Council of Örebro (1529) "that the simple clerics and church pastors might have some guidance in God's Holy Word." The work was so simply conceived, stated the preface, that if the little postil were merely read to the people by rote it would bear fruit.

Petri wished through this postil to encourage the use of Scripture; his foreword began with thanksgiving and praise for God's great gift in making His word available in understandable Swedish. In a special exhortation to pastors, he emphasized that it is the message concerning salvation which must be drawn out of the Bible. This scriptural teaching is to be included within the context of the service.

The Latin mass was still chanted in most of the Swedish churches during the era when this postil was written, and the intention of the postil was certainly that the vernacular sermon with its introduction should have its place within the context of the mass. What was the relation of the Swedish mass, for which Olaus Petri presented a model order in 1531, to the sermon? This is a disputed and intricate question. We know that the Swedish mass did not make provision for preaching and that Olaus Petri seemed to recommend continuous lections from the Bible instead of the pericopes. Was this an expression of his real attitude? It is difficult to believe that the author of this postil could so soon after its publication have thought that the pericopes should be abrogated. How could simple clerics interpret the books of the Bible serially? Details may be interpreted in various ways, but the difficulties can most easily be solved if we assume that the Swedish mass of 1531 was intended as a low communion mass, probably designed for weekdays. As the Swedish mass replaced the Latin high mass, it must have undergone revision: place must have been given to the liturgical chants (which remained Latin for a long time), to the accepted texts, and to preaching. These developments were relatively stabilized in the 1541 edition of the Swedish mass.

Although most Swedish homiletical literature during the Reformation was translated, Olaus Petri's postil confronts us as an original work which bears the imprint of the author's personality. Sufficient recognition has too seldom been given to this unique contribution. Perhaps this is to some degree because of the postil's unpretentious simplicity. It is, however, precisely here that the master's hand is apparent. The unpretentious matter-of-factness which characterizes all of Petri's writings is the highest type of art. No model existed for Petri's postil. In German, only Luther's *Church Postil* was available, and Petri was in conscious opposition to it, for its spirit was in large measure foreign to him. Nor did Petri accept the *Church Postil* as a model with respect to form. Olaus Petri's sermons are moderately long, and every sermon contains two parts, the first reproducing the text with explanatory comments and the second coming to grips with the "teaching": the conclusion is a short *votum* or a doxology. This type of sermon is reminiscent of the medieval sermon in its simplest form. At the same time, however, we cannot find a better illustration of the distance between medieval and Reformation piety than appears when a sermon from one of the Vadstena postils is contrasted to one of Olaus Petri's expositions. This is especially true with respect to the use of the Bible, for any such contrast will give Olaus Petri a place of honor among the biblical expositors of the Reformation age. Throughout, marks of artistry appear in unstudied simplicity to make the postil one of the great monuments in the history of the Swedish language, more accessible to contemporary readers than a great deal of the literature written and printed in Sweden during the two subsequent centuries.

The postil had a pedagogical purpose, seeking to be a school and reportorium for preachers. It is hardly to be considered an example of Olaus Petri's own preaching. Evidence indicates that his oral presentation was far more filled with spirit and fire, and that he possessed prophetic characteristics not obvious in the postil. This conclusion can be drawn from the two sermonic treatises which are available to us, the coronation sermon of 1528 and the sermon on oaths, of 1539.

The Church Orders of George Norman and Laurentius Petri

The Vadstena Articles of 1522 prescribed that candidates for the ministry were to be diligently trained in preaching. A great contribution to homiletics in Sweden was made by a German-born protegé of Gustavus I, George Norman (d. 1553), who revived pastoral training in the crumbling diocesan chapters by establishing theological lectorships in the diocesan cities. Norman also gave final shape to the first evangelical guide to preaching to be published in Sweden, his *Short Introduction* (1549), written in German and translated into Swedish, which gave homiletical and theological rules, as well as practical hints, worthy of emulation by preachers in any era. This little guide exhibited some influence from Melanchthon, but Norman distinguished himself from Melanchthon by his independence, his practical orientation, and his profitable use of the humanistic homiletical theories which had been developed in Germany. He refers to Erasmus' *Ecclesiastes* and to Augustine's *De Doctrina Christiana* but considers them more specifically related to rhetoric in the schools than to the office of preaching in the church.

In the areas of pastoral training and preaching, Laurentius Petri (1499-1573) was in accord with George Norman. Petri, the first evangelical Archbishop of Uppsala and the younger brother of Olaus, was a great liturgical specialist of the Reformation who did not neglect preaching. Many of his writings are homiletical in character. His postil, published in four volumes in 1555, did not pretend to be an original composition. It has been suggested by some scholars that this work was a translation of Veit Dietrich's *Kinderpostille* of 1546; more recent investigations have established, however, that Laurentius did not use Dietrich uncritically and that he did in fact use material from Luther's postils. He sought to follow the church year in accordance with Swedish usage and to present expositions for those saints' days which were still observed. His postil, which was widely used, became the basic source for the unlettered parish pastors for more than fifty years. It was reprinted in 1630 and 1641.

Laurentius Petri presented his thoughts on preaching in several contexts. In a pastoral letter (1558) he spoke of the responsibilities of the preacher: In the rural areas he should preach one half-hour on the catechism and use the other half-hour to interpret the Gospel for the day, a prescription which is repeated in the *Church Order* (1571). At a meeting of pastors in 1566, Laurentius made a presentation of the preacher's duties which bore the marks of his humanistic learning. None of these suggestions, however, obscured the clear policies which were to be established in the directions to the *Church Order* of 1571. The two introductory chapters of the *Church Order*, "On Preaching and Christian Teaching" and "Order in Preaching," are most important. These directions concerning the external structure of the sermon and its place in the service build upon Olaus Petri and the tradition developed around him. The preacher is to speak on the Gospel of the mass and not on any legends concerning the saints; in case some legend related to the day is in accord with Scripture, however, it may be briefly considered. Preachers in the cities must preach on the Epistle at vespers, a time when the catechism has no place. This is also true of matins. If the Epistle is not used on Sunday it should be considered on the days of prayer during the week; otherwise, the pastor should preach serially on the whole books of the Bible. During Holy Week the history of the passion of Christ should be interpreted. An hour, which is a "suitable time" for the sermon, must also allow time for the introductory and final exhortations and the prayer following the sermon, "otherwise if it is made so long that the people begin to suffer, very little fruit will follow." A formula is given for the introductory exhortation to prayer ending with the Our Father. Following this, a hymn of prayer or praise should be sung. As the text is read the congregation rises. The announcements of mass, exhortations to prayer, the prayers, and the confession of sin and absolution follow the sermon.

These general rules, with variations made necessary by the times, have been repeated and made effective in the law of the Church of Sweden. They surely have had a wholesome influence on Swedish preaching through the centuries and preserved it from the one-sidedness of fashions. The decisions in the *Church Order* are complemented rather than revised in the *Nova Ordinantia* of 1575. Here, however, we notice more of humanism, an influence which seems to have been consciously forced into the background in the *Church Order*. The liturgical context appears more clearly. We note with interest that the sermon in the Swedish mass had until this time preceded the chanting of the creed, but that the order was now to be reversed. In certain quarters where some worshipers made it their disagreeable custom to leave church immediately after the sermon, they were to be seriously exhorted from the pulpit to remain "both when the prayers are made and when the Blessed Sacrament is celebrated."

We do not possess any homiletical documents from these decades of agitated liturgical strife. Certainly the weapon of preaching must have been used diligently by all sides and measured exposition must many times have given way to flaming polemic. If sources were available, the picture of preaching during the Reformation in Sweden would take on more color and shading. As it is, we must be satisfied to confirm the fact that sermonizing in this period, by its faithful attachment to the pericopes and its thorough integration into the service, especially high mass, was given a liturgical setting which greatly influenced its inner structure. The task of exegeting the text was taken with great seriousness. Pedagogical and doctrinal elements gave very little room for the prophetic. Most preachers were content to reproduce their sermon helps in a very dependent way. Preaching methods inherited from the Middle Ages had been forgotten, and as yet it is not possible to trace any dependence upon the techniques of German homiletics. The era of German influence would soon dawn.

The Seventeenth Century

The period which begins with the Council of Uppsala in 1593 and ends near the close of the seventeenth century, called for want of a better name the period of orthodoxy, has in many respects been given less scholarly attention than any other period in Swedish church history. As a result, it is possible to present only a preliminary sketch of preaching during this time.

It is, perhaps, easiest to survey the period immediately following the meeting at Uppsala. Material is very restricted and consists chiefly of reproductions of German homiletical models. Theological education at higher levels, especially in *gymnasia,* began at this time to insist on higher standards and greater audacity in preaching, but to the degree that an independent homiletical production appeared in Sweden during the time of orthodoxy, it stood under the dominant influence of German prototypes.

From the time of Petrus Jonae Angermannus (1559-1630), Bishop of Vǎxjö, to the 1680's, homiletical sources grew very rapidly. Yet the large quantity of printed material is inadequate as a source of knowledge for the actual content of the proclamation. The literature is dominated by sermons which were, according to the custom of the time, ornamented with re-worked and expanded dedications and embellishments.[9] The Swedish preacher of the seventeenth century was given countless opportunities to proclaim the word of God, and with these opportunities came many temptations to gild the word with human endeavor. The ordinary requirements of speaking, especially in city parishes, were exacting enough, but in addition to the Sunday service, vespers and matins were held on days of prayer at which preaching was then expected serially to follow the books of the Bible. In addition, there were also catechetical and passion sermons. Special demands were added to these usual duties, foremost among them being funeral sermons, in all eras the most delicate form of homiletic production. It is not an exaggeration to state that more than half of the sources available from this era are funeral sermons.

In addition to funerals, all sorts of events in the lives of distinguished people became occasions for devotional meditations. These, with the entire literature of casual addresses from this period, comprise a very interesting source of investigation for the historian of culture. It may be sufficient merely to list the categories which make up this literature: triumph and thanksgiving sermons for victories and peace, sermons on folk holidays, sermons in the Swedish legislature, sermons in district courts, and sermons in the market place. Events in the church and in the life of the congregation, especially church dedications and

---

[9] A sermon by Petrus Eschilli, preached in 1635, is a good example. It fills nearly one hundred pages, presents subheadings in Greek, boasts much scholarly ostentation, and concludes with a series of congratulations addressed to well-known men.

anniversaries of pastoral service, were also celebrated with preaching.

While all these homiletical specialties are abundantly present in the literature, the ordinary Sunday sermon remains very poorly represented. Especially noteworthy is the absence of postils. We are thus poorly informed about the ordinary proclamation which was heard in the parish churches during these years. We can draw some conclusions, however, from the directions and exhortations that are given for preaching, and from the criticisms that are available. To gain a firm grasp of the oral sermon during the seventeenth century, it would be necessary to make a thorough inventory of all extant handwritten sources.

We know that Swedish theological study during this century gave special emphasis to the task of training preachers. In the *gymnasia* as well as in the universities, *collegia concionatoria* were held. When the Diocese of Västerås requested that a professor in practical theology be elected the request was turned down because "the total study of theology is practical." Nevertheless, such a professorship was established at the University of Uppsala in 1686 with Israel Kolmodin (1643-1709) as the first incumbent. In their instruction the professors were aware of the homiletical theories which had been developed at the German university, and many German handbooks were used. The influence of these, together with the indigenous tradition, was of crucial importance in the development of preaching. German homiletical theory gained disciples in Sweden and these disciples characteristically gave a moderate application to the orthodox technical apparatus which had been inherited from the Middle Ages. In the later years of the century, it is evident, the art of preaching was studied and practiced with seriousness and concern. The ability to create independent sermons, lacking in the sixteenth century, had now become common. The task of the preacher was highly respected.

In general it is an impossible task to differentiate the varying homiletical tendencies before 1680. Individual differences were certainly present—theological orientations, in spite of the tendency toward confessional uniformity, exhibited some variation; the disparate needs of different audiences left their traces. All, however, lived in the spiritual climate of orthodoxy and to a greater or lesser degree followed its homiletical directions.

Although it is hazardous to build an analysis of the Swedish sermon during the period of orthodoxy with so few available sources, several traits are apparent. The liturgical context did not leave particularly strong traces in the texts of the sermons themselves, but in the case of sermons at high mass the context is self-evident. The use of a hymn related to the message of the day, following the *exordium,* helped to tie the sermon to the rest of the service. It was already possible to discern a tendency for the sermon itself to become a liturgical rubric, since the formal language of worship had begun to overshadow the living witness.

We may not dispute the fact that the preachers of the seventeenth century wished to be expositors of the Bible. Biblicism was apparent, albeit often misdirected—an abundant use of proof texts being no guarantee of a biblical spirit.

Original prophetic contributions were few. Here we think primarily of Isak Rothovius (1572-1652) and Johannes Rudbeckius (1581-1646). We cannot deny that orthodoxy's preaching did have a specific address to its own time. Preaching was an influence not only in the parish but also in the history of the nation. A prophetic consciousness of call is found in Rudbeckius' sermon of judgment against Gustavus Adolphus in 1617, one of the noble documents in the history of Swedish preaching. An energetic preaching of the law was certainly motivated by the situation of the people and often assumed concrete form. Exhortations to repentance were no empty declarations but rather were characterized by an urgent desire to waken sinners to a living consciousness of their state. The background for preaching in this era was an eschatological perspective which possessed a fearsome actuality both for the speaker and for his hearers. The last decade of the seventeenth century was a time of transition. Students often speak of a new style of preaching which began to appear then, but it is not easy to establish the nature of this new proclamation. It is easier to detect some of the movements which influenced the new development. One of these was the older pietism, which created a negative reaction to objective, formal preaching.

Two personalities dominated the latter half of the seventeenth century. Haquin Spegel (1645-1714) continued the tradition of orthodoxy. A new spirit of renewal and exuberance comes to our attention in Jesper Swedberg (1653-1735), who is the more extensively represented in homiletical literature, especially by his postils. His expositions, generally analytical, are interspersed with all sorts of capriciously inserted exhortations and descriptions of the age. In spite of his freedom from slavish form, his exuberant originality and his criticism of the excesses of pietism, Swedberg remained a child of the seventeenth century even though his span of life continued into the eighteenth.

The Eighteenth Century

J. Christopher Stricker (1726-92), in his preface to the postil of Abraham Petterson, accurately described the situation of preaching in eighteenth-century Sweden:

If we have plenty of anything here in this world it is certainly the preaching of the word of God. Here we hear preaching early and late, in town and in country. There is no ear which can hear but that it has the opportunity of hearing God's word: there is no eye which can see but that it has the opportunity of reading God's word. Here God's word is proclaimed by writing and by speaking, publicly and privately, on holy days and every day. Babes in arms are carried to the house of God in order that they may become accustomed to hear the word of God in due time, and the aged could easier count the gray hairs on their heads than the exact number of all the sermons which they have heard during their lifetime.[10]

One cannot penetrate deeply into this literature without being impressed by the concern the preachers evidenced for their task. Technical training continued and the demands on preaching were sharpened by the pietistic movement, which was able to make its influence felt even among those who did not share its fervor. The dedication with which the preachers of the era gave themselves to their task found its reward in the respect their hearers accorded them.

During this era the whole history of the Church of Sweden must be delineated against the background of German Lutheranism. This is also true of preaching. There was contact with the oratory of French classicism and with Tillotson's new style of preaching, but homiletical theory was preponderantly mediated through Germany. A synthesis of the homiletical style of the scholastic tradition, pietism's zeal for the care of souls, and the demands of the new era for clarity and simplicity was attempted by J. J. Rambach (1693-1735) in Germany. This synthesis was adopted and further developed in Sweden during the latter half of the eighteenth century, and has continued to be an influence of extreme importance in Swedish preaching to the present; it therefore occupies a unique place in the history of Christian preaching.

No significant preacher of the eighteenth century was able to ignore the demands for personal decision, for religious intimacy and warmth, which were found in pietism. Similarly, none of the best preachers was able to ignore the demands of the emerging Enlightenment for logical clarity and a more transparent vocabulary. Sven Baelter (1713-60), Abraham Petterson (1724-64), and Anders Nohrborg (1725-67), who were subject

---

[10] Abraham Petterson, *I Jesu Namn! Christelige Predikningar, hallne öfwer de Årliga Sön-och Högtids-dagars Evangelier* (Stockholm, 1764).

to these demands, represent the zenith of the culture of the time.

Baelter, the oldest of the three, was only forty-seven years old when he died as dean of Växjö. Pietism, the Moravian Brethren, the moderate Enlightenment, the German homiletical literature, and the works of Tillotson in German translation were all factors in his development. His *Historical Notes on Church Ceremonies* is the first attempt to give a scholarly presentation of the Swedish service. The basic tone of his preaching was the union of the soul with Christ. This emphasis was derived from pietism and the Moravians; logical clarity was derived from the philosophy of Leibnitz and Wolff. His style was developed in keeping with the movements of the time; it flowed easily with a certain dignified elegance, indicating his appreciation of the literary value of the Bible. Nature also was a subject for his preaching, but without the excesses of the later years of the Enlightenment.

We see the currents of the age more clearly and directly in Abraham Petterson, who became court preacher for King Adolf Fredrik at the age of twenty-three. He left behind him material for a tremendous postil of at least a thousand pages which was printed in six editions. Evaluations of Petterson have varied. He certainly did not possess the timelessness of Baelter or Nohrborg; both his orthodox zeal and his Wolffian demonstrations make him less palatable than they to modern readers. His zeal for apologetic and his wordy expositions on nature took on the color of his own era in a remarkable way. Finally, no preacher before Petterson so zealously used Rambach's method of homiletical address.

Anders Nohrborg's unpretentious personality rises above all other preachers in this era. Few dramatic events are found in his life; only a small number of letters give us a glimpse behind the veil and an insight into his tragedies. When, toward the time of his death, tuberculosis was so far advanced that he was not able to preach, Nohrborg taught those around him "the order of salvation" and conversed about the publication of his dear postil, a task which was not yet complete. He died in 1767 at the age of forty-two. The projected plan for *The Order of Salvation for Fallen Man,* which his heirs had difficulty in publishing, was printed four years later, in 1771. It is certainly his own work and it was carefully edited by his brother Daniel.

Contemporary readers who set themselves the task of reading *The Order of Salvation* without being intimidated by its dimensions, cannot escape asking first of all why this book became so beloved, as indeed it sometimes still is. It was published in its twentieth edition in 1932 and is occasionally still given as a present to catechumens in sections of Sweden with an "old church" emphasis. The systematic construction is almost fearsome: The sermons are loosed from their connection with the church year and are placed within the scheme of the order of salvation. The first sermon belongs to the Day of the Annunciation; the last sermon in Part Nine belongs to Candlemas. It is evident that the author was scarcely aware of the significance of the liturgical context of preaching, for the concentration is typically individualistic. At the same time, however, it is true that the objective fact of atonement and justification has seldom been presented more energetically, not to say more one-sidedly. The special pietistic unction of the book is not consonant with the rugged clarity which is coldly dominant.

Nohrborg stood in the tradition of Rambach but was less influenced by pietism. This is evident in his use of the same preaching method as Rambach, even though he did not generally use the threefold application, often preferring a summary. He used the Bible zealously, but he was not primarily a biblical expositor. His stringent schematic arrangements made the *exordium* more dominant than the text. It is primarily as a result of Nohrborg's influence that the correspondence between the *exordium* and the theme, often at the expense of the text, has become a prominent trait in conservative preaching in Sweden.

With the publication in 1779 of *An Essay Concerning the Right Method of Preaching* by Johan Möller (1738-1805), the Bishop of Visby, an ideal for preaching was enunciated which the author believed had already been attained in Nohrborg's postil. This work, the only thorough handbook in homiletics which appeared in Sweden during the eighteenth century, contributed mightily toward giving Nohrborg's work a kind of canonical status. Such preaching, therefore, was enabled both to outlive the stormy floods of Enlightenment rhetoric and to become an essential influence in the homiletical development of the nineteenth century. Even today, Möller's book is pleasant reading. It made orthodoxy, which was the basic note in its proclamation, warm and intimate and gave it a form which possessed some of the clarity and elegance of the Enlightenment. The preaching exemplified by Nohrborg and motivated by Möller is one of the most important mileposts in the history of more recent preaching in Sweden.

Möller emphasized that a sermon is not to be an academic lecture. He warned against an "affected, inflated and vain oratory, which is much less usable when it deals with spiritual subjects since the ultimate purpose is hindered rather than helped." He realized that spiritual oratory requires a rhetoric of its own and therefore he cautioned against the use of French and English sources since "French sermons (usually Catholic) contain only moralistic subjects, and are developed on a false and insufficient foundation and preached in very poor style; and in English preaching nowadays we find little more than a natural theology and a moralistic doctrinal structure."

In the life of the Church of Sweden, the Enlightenment was significant for the development of preaching since it represented the first invasion of the traditional pattern of orthodoxy, the first of the movements which would challenge the supremacy of the classical sermon. Bishop Magnus Lehnberg (1758-1808) was the most brilliant of the preachers influenced by the Swedish

Enlightenment. The old proclamation of law and gospel, of sin and grace, was beginning to be pushed aside by an emotional moralism. A melancholy spirit was in the process of being transformed into a bright optimism.

At the age of thirty-six, Lehnberg became pastor in Stockholm and a member of the Swedish Academy. There he won a unique reputation as a pulpit orator. There is a strange contrast between the praise that was heaped upon Lehnberg by his contemporaries and the evaluation of subsequent generations. One contemporary compared Lehnberg with the great masters of French preaching and praised him as the ideal orator: "Flying higher, if this expression is applicable to an orator, than Fléchier: clear, mellow and stirring like Massillon: rich and descriptive like Fénelon. Lehnberg, in common with the latter, has become one of the more recent preachers who has reached the same perfection in style and presentation as the great orators of Athens and Rome." Archbishop J. A. Lindblom sought to explain the huge audiences which Lehnberg enjoyed: "No church was large enough when he preached, as long as he ministered in Stockholm; people were in danger of being choked by the crowds; the doors had to be shut in the face of the stream of people who pushed from the outside." Lindblom concluded that the explanation for this lay in the fact that in contrast to the usual method of preaching, Lehnberg appealed to the intellect as well as to the emotions and constantly found the way to the will through reason and the response of man's whole being.

Lehnberg stands as the best example of those Swedish preachers who, as a result of the influences of secular rhetoric, lost some of their feeling for the independence and uniqueness of the sermon. The sermon became a religious address without any real relation to the liturgy; it became a declamation on an edifying and moving subject, not the exposition of a text. Yet even though Lehnberg's preaching did fail to accomplish its essential purpose as preaching—no doubt the reason it became obsolete so quickly—it was a useful and provocative reaction against the stale traditionalism which is one of the perpetual dangers of churchly preaching.

A great distance separates Lehnberg and Henrik Schartau (1757-1825), who was not well-known among his contemporaries. There is no doubt now as to which of the two is the more relevant to modern times. Schartau was just as exclusively a representative of southern Sweden as Lehnberg was of northern Sweden; he contributed more than anyone else to giving southern and western Sweden a clearly delineated religious individuality.

Schartau was first discovered as a preacher by a wider public only after his death. Collections of his works have appeared, but the extant handwritten sources have not all been published. It is generally recognized that the most important sources are the *Thirteen Sermons* which were published in 1831, and the large collection of "sermons of which the greater number have more complete outlines" in four volumes (1830-1843).[11]

No other Swedish preacher has survived in a "school" to the same extent as Schartau. Even those who are strangers to the tradition which stems from him, or who feel repelled by the ruggedness of his presentation or the logical exactitude of his schemata, must acknowledge that Schartau is one of the greatest figures in the more recent history of Swedish preaching. And to the same degree that we become engrossed in his writings we cannot escape being captivated by this preacher's deep concern for souls and by his deep knowledge of the secrets of the heart.

The classical Swedish sermon, which had been best represented in the eighteenth century by Baelter and Nohrborg, appeared

---

[11] [A biography and translation of fifteen of Schartau's sermons is available in English in S. G. Högglund, *Henric Schartau and the Order of Grace* (Rock Island, Ill.: Augustana Book Concern, 1928).—TRANSLATOR.]

once again in Schartau. It was his influence that gave this type of sermon sufficient status to justify its being called classical. He was also, doubtless, influenced by Möller, whose basic concepts he applied to an astonishing degree.

Schartau contributed toward a stiff dignity in later Swedish preaching which is often considered by the present generation to be a heavy burden. In him we detect a tendency which has also appeared in some of his disciples, to make the sermon into a liturgical act. This is the obverse side of a conscious attempt to preserve the spirit of worshipful devotion and to differentiate preaching from the secular address.

Schartau's principles of biblical interpretation would require a separate investigation. Very few teachers of the church have bound their hearers so closely to Scripture. For him it was self-evident that the message of Scripture was one message, salvation in Jesus Christ. The biblical word has an errand to every soul and its truth is confirmed in the experience of every man who has placed himself under its discipline and followed its precepts. There is therefore a singular correspondence between the word and the needs of the believing soul. This presupposition, basic for the edifying use of the Bible, was for Schartau the axiom which summarized both his exegesis and his prophetic message.

Schartau's contact with the Moravians, which gave him an abhorrence for all sentimentality, also gave his love for Jesus a special intimacy and his longing for union with the Savior a warmth which the sober restraint of his utterances could not completely conceal. His intellectualism, the apparently cold clarity which knew no short cuts to the human heart that by-passed reason, came from the Enlightenment. To establish the elements which have been incorporated and blended into his preaching is not to depreciate his originality. These elements have been merged into a new and living unity and bear the stamp of his personality, a personality whose power is even more clearly evident because he constantly sought to remain in the background for the sake of the message.

During the first decades of the nineteenth century, Swedish preaching oscillated between the two poles which are symbolized by Lehnberg and Schartau. The romantic mood, both in literature and theology, brought with it a new appreciation of popular piety and a new respect for that which was old. An appreciation of the classical sermon was evident among the preachers who had become aware of this mood. J. O. Wallin (1779-1839) was one of these. In 1814 he wrote: "It is time that the old again gains the respect it has lost. We have heard Voltaire preach long enough: it is time that Luther again is heard. I often read Petterson and Baelter before I go into the pulpit."

In several respects Wallin's work formed a brilliant conclusion to the era characterized by tension between Enlightenment rhetoric and the classical Swedish sermon. He consciously strove for a synthesis of the two. As an orator he gained his chief following by his use of the legacy from Lehnberg. The spiritual fare in his sermons now appears to be rather meager. What is merely stirring occupies too much space. A civically oriented moralism frequently asserts itself, and sin and grace are very often ideas rather than spiritual realities. The platonic-humanistic orientation did not leave room for the full tragic realism of Christianity.

Wallin's preaching, however, did have homiletical merit in other respects. He did have an ear for the peculiar cadence of the word of Scripture. His sermons are somewhat more exegetical than either Nohrborg's or Schartau's. The liturgical element in the sermon, long forgotten or ignored, was again given a rightful place. The diligent use of hymn verses, especially those of his own composing, was a bond that united the sermon and the liturgy; indeed, some have attempted to characterize Wallin's sermons as disembodied hymns.

The Nineteenth Century

One significant factor in the development of nineteenth-century Swedish preaching was the homiletical instruction imparted by the theological faculties who now were in charge of the training of pastors. This training, especially at the University of Lund, contributed toward conserving and widening the classical type of sermon which now appeared in modern dress. Various influences at Uppsala, some of which were low church in character, tended to cancel one another. This homiletical development was basically determined by influences from other countries, especially from Germany; the Swedish contributions were noticeably few and unoriginal. The tremendous number of sermons from other countries which were translated during this century were more important than homiletical theory, the influence of which was not especially profound. A stronger wave of Scandinavian influences first appeared toward the end of the century and grew to larger proportions during the first decades of the twentieth century.

The impact of Anglo-Saxon devotional and homiletical literature was extensive. Among the Anglican preachers, only F. W. Robertson became generally known in Sweden. The American Unitarians, Channing, Priestly, and Parker, exerted a great influence on the growing liberalism of the mid-century, but in clerical circles they were uniformly regarded as dangerous heretics. Puritan and Nonconformist literature, of English and American origin, was much more influential and inundated the country in the 1860's. The doors were opened for this development by the lay evangelist, C. O. Rosenius (1816-68), who diligently used materials from Baxter, Bunyan, and others. Approximately twenty collections of Charles Haddon Spurgeon's sermons have been published in Sweden, and Dwight L. Moody's writings have also been widely circulated. This great influx of Anglo-

Saxon literature was to a large degree mediated by the free church movement. The impact of foreign homiletical literature on Swedish preaching during the nineteenth century was not so great as the quantity of imported and translated material would lead us to expect, but these influences did work together with other factors in making the nineteenth-century homiletical development exceedingly complicated.

The most evident of all developments during this era was doubtless the one which emanated from Schartau and was continued by his disciples in the Diocese of Gothenburg. There may be different opinions as to the value of this tradition, but it has clearly contributed to the common consciousness, among both preachers and lay people, of the uniqueness of the sermon.

The vigorous revival movements of these generations are often associated with the preaching of Peter Wieselgren (1800-1877), who possessed highly original gifts and who could, in his extemporaneous preaching, rise to real oratorical heights. He often, however, united his brilliance with bizarre traits which served to detract from his lasting effectiveness. Wieselgren is an example both of the new revivalism and of the new interest in missions, and he united the romantic traits of the era with influences from the English-speaking world.

The new biblicism of the nineteenth century appeared in its full power in Peter Fjellstedt (1802-1881). As few preachers before him, he made the Scriptures speak. This biblicism was further expanded in Rosenius' untutored but brilliant biblical preaching which, as a result of the evangelical revival, became exceedingly significant for Swedish preaching during the late nineteenth century.[12] This type of preaching appeared in an

[12] [C. O. Rosenius, *The Believer Free from the Law,* trans. Adolf Hult (Rock Island, Ill.: Augustana Book Concern, 1923). A summary of Rosenius' religious development and influence is to be found in G. Everett Arden, *Four Northern Lights* (Minneapolis: Augsburg, 1964), pp. 115-48.—TRANSLATOR.]

even more pronounced form in the uncommonly great popular oratory of P. P. Waldenström (1838-1917).[13]

The common characteristics of preaching in the Swedish free churches are: biblicism, a dominance of the revival motif, an artless form freed from all technical restraints, and strong influences from English and American homiletical and devotional literature. The sermon in the Swedish free churches has derived its bold, often direct style of presentation, as well as its spirit of exultation in salvation, from these sources. The latter spirit has been especially true of the Pentecostal movement and its foremost representatives, Lewi Pethrus (born 1884) and Sven Lidman (1882-1960). Here we are able to detect the beginnings of a type of liturgical creation in an otherwise highly unliturgical oratory. Lidman is one of the best examples in the history of Christendom of one who makes masterly and perfect literary use of a preaching style with medieval origins. As a result of influences from the Anglo-Saxon world, Swedish revival preaching has sometimes found it necessary to make room for an ethical and social proclamation similar to that which has occupied such a prominent place in more recent American preaching. Besides these traits, which are derived from non-Swedish sources, we can also detect in free church preaching a certain dependence upon the liturgical tradition. In the Swedish Mission Covenant Church, for example, it is customary to make the established pericope for the day the source of the sermon. The liturgical element thus becomes effective in a religious community which has in principle dismissed it.

The line of demarcation between the Church of Sweden and the free churches was often unclear in the days of the evangelical revival. A partial synthesis between the classical homiletical

---

[13] [Waldenström was the founder of the Swedish Mission Covenant Church both in Sweden and in the United States. The denomination has a separate identity in America, where since 1957 it has been known as the Evangelical Covenant Church in America.—TRANSLATOR.]

tradition and the personally oriented piety of the revivals can be seen in Gottfrid Billing (1841-1925), Bishop of Våsterås, whose preaching stood as a model for a whole generation of pastors.

The Renewal of Churchly Preaching

Low church biblicism rejected the critical study of the Bible which at the end of the nineteenth century had introduced a new ferment in the work of the theological faculties and, by degrees, also in the work of the church. In the free church world this attitude of opposition has not yet been overcome. Disquiet also appeared in the church in the face of the negative orientation and defiant self-confidence of the new exegesis, and this tended to hinder biblical preaching for a time. The old method of interpretation continued to be used, but with mixed feelings and a bad conscience. In this context a significant contribution was made by Fredrik Fehr (1849-95) and his disciple and friend, S. A. Fries (1867-1914), both of whom attempted to use the new theology in the service of devotion. They stood under the influence of the religious idealism of Pontus Wikner (1837-88). Wikner never became a pastor but his sermons for young students are part of the classic devotional literature of Sweden.

The renewal of preaching which marked the first decades of the twentieth century was derived from several sources. Doubtless one source was the new view of the Bible which had arisen out of the confusion of the liberal era and which had matured and deepened so that exegesis and homiletics could again be friends. At this point much still remains to be done. The basic orientation of biblical research, that the texts of the New Testament can only be understood as confession and kerygma and thus as fragments of preaching, is an opportunity which present-day preaching has utilized only to a limited degree. This exegetical orientation also includes the deepened and crucial insight that the church itself is an essential part of the gospel.

The rediscovery of the church was one of the most prominent characteristics of the Young Church Movement which swept the Church of Sweden in the early decades of this century. This crusade, which had received impulses from the student movements and also from Danish and Norwegian church life and through them from the revivalistic piety of the nineteenth century, played a significant role in later Swedish preaching. The Young Church Movement addressed people as groups rather than as individuals; it desired both to speak the language of the time and to renew the historic forms of worship. The preaching of J. A. Eklund (1863-1945), Bishop of Karlstad, was of great importance for the structuring of this movement, especially the preaching which marked his earlier ministry in the cathedral church at Uppsala. These sermons continue to be the crusade's primary historical monument; in the estimation of many he above all others revived Swedish preaching. He belonged to the generation which personally struggled with the problem of a new view of the Bible. He spoke to people and to the community with a strong, sometimes reckless prophetic consciousness. Especially important was the new appreciation of and joy in the holy ordinances of the church which appeared in Eklund's preaching: the shifting seasons of the church year and the solemn, formal language of the liturgy were made into living resources as never before in the history of Swedish preaching. Classical homiletical technique appeared in the demand for order and clear division, while the *exordium* most often disappeared.

In addition to the Young Church Movement, which stemmed from Eklund, and the tradition of western Sweden which wished to preserve the legacy from Schartau, we notice a third group of preachers which attempted to preserve its independence. The members of this group consciously allied themselves with both

213

the piety of the "old church" revivals and the classical preaching pattern, and to both they gave a new actuality. Bishop Victor Rundgren (1869-1936) and Bishop Sam Stadener (1872-1937) worthily represented this tradition. These preachers, however, like those from western Sweden, left the impression that the twentieth-century crisis in theology had passed them and their preaching by without traces.

Bishop Einar Billing (1871-1914) lives in the grateful memory of his hearers to a greater extent than could be concluded from the few examples which have been published.[14] His preaching was characterized by a grappling with biblical texts which seemed to continue even during the oral presentation. He often made well-known passages of Scripture shine with new brilliance as unexpected treasures were revealed. Billing has had few equals in evangelical Christianity as a preacher to students.

A survey of the development of Swedish preaching should not ignore the name of Nathanael Beskow (1865-1953). Few contemporary devotional authors in Sweden have had a larger circle of readers than this lay preacher from Djursholm had. He was the foremost Swedish representative of the sermonic essay which was perfected on Anglo-Saxon soil. He was, however, a stranger to the newly awakened consciousness of the church.

This consciousness of the church stands as the most significant difference between Beskow and Archbishop Nathan Söderblom (1866-1931). Söderblom's preaching modified the general Swedish style of preaching in many respects. He cannot be placed in a special group or school since he used no traditional technique. His extraordinary talents were, however, dedicated

---

[14] [The only work by Billing available in English is *Our Calling*, a discussion of Christian vocation translated by Conrad Bergendoff (Philadelphia: Fortress Press, 1965). Cf. Conrad Bergendoff's essay, "The Ethical Thought of Einar Billing" in Philip J. Hefner (ed.). *The Scope of Grace: Essays in Honor of Joseph Sittler* (Philadelphia: Fortress Press, 1964), pp. 279-306.—TRANSLATOR.]

wholly to the service of the church. He understood and stated the new views concerning the church earlier and more clearly than any of his contemporaries. Penetrating exegesis and a clear understanding of critical problems, prophetic zeal and liturgical understanding—all were present in his preaching. Those who remember his sermons in Holy Trinity Church in Uppsala still wonder how his informal and unconventional style could be fused into the liturgical context. This is a reminder that preaching does not achieve its purpose in the service if it does not remain a nonliturgical infusion into the liturgically oriented cult.

In the present situation the renewal of churchly preaching in Sweden is perhaps more a program and a hope than an experienced reality. New demands clamor for recognition. The impatience with stereotyped preaching which does not seem to meet our present generation is often expressed vehemently. This dissatisfaction is itself a testimony to the significance preaching always possesses or should possess. The great prophets whom the age demands have not yet appeared. New tones in preaching are needed; yet preaching cannot neglect the past without hurting itself.

Preaching, not least preaching in Sweden, brings an exhortation to work and to faithfulness. It places before us a responsible inheritance and gives us unique resources to conserve. As the preacher competes with the other demands of the age, his demands upon himself are sharpened and he also gains a heightened respect for the task which has been assigned to him, a task shared by Augustine, Luther, Wesley, Nohrborg and Schartau. As long as ordinary men are given the absurd responsibility of preaching Sunday after Sunday the need for method and technique will not cease to exist. The prophetic gift is not bound by any rules. Nevertheless, every preacher of God's word is in duty bound, to the best of his ability, within the context of the services of the church and in the humble spirit of devotion demanded by all worship, to interpret that eternal message for the people of every age.

Annotated Bibliography on the History of Preaching

by MORRIS J. NIEDENTHAL

The attempt to compile an accessible and useful bibliography in the area of the history of preaching is revealing. It shows the paucity of recent material on the subject in comparison, for example, with nineteenth-century material. In addition, it shows how the role of the preacher among his people has changed. We are not apt to think of preachers today in terms of princes, kings, and ambassadors of the pulpit. The images we use are more modest, less majestic, and less individualistic. The decline of what might be called a romanticized view of preachers and preaching may partially explain that dissipation of interest in the history of preaching which has characterized most of this century.

Whatever the explanation, a corrective is needed. The situation of the pulpit today cannot be correctly understood apart from its past. The following bibliography is offered as an aid into that past. It includes general surveys, specialized studies, and popular works somewhat dramatic and inspirational in character.

GENERAL SURVEY

Broadus, J. A. *Lectures on the History of Preaching*. New York: A. C. Armstrong and Son, 1896. First written in 1876, a brief survey that concentrates on the way preachers have related themselves to their time. Although the work is stamped by a romanticized view of the preacher (e.g., "he is a born ruler of mankind") it contains a helpful chapter on the French preachers of the seventeenth century.

Dargan, E. C. *A History of Preaching*. Grand Rapids, Mich.: Baker Book House, 1954. First published in 1905, this is still a basic work, unequaled in giving a framework of names, dates, and biographies. It covers the field from biblical times to the beginning of the twentieth century. The lack of adequate theological analysis and criticism is regrettable, but this two-volume work still introduces the field better than any other.

Ker, J. *Lectures on the History of Preaching.* London: Hodder & Stoughton, 1888. Gives sketches of celebrated preachers including their views on preaching and specimens of their work. Over half of the volume is devoted to preachers of the Reformation and post-Reformation periods in Germany. The author's own bias shows in an excellent chapter on Spener.

Pattison, T. H. *The History of Christian Preaching.* Philadelphia: The American Baptist Publication Society, 1903. Aims to show how the voice of the preacher has been a power in the world from the days of the apostles until the twentieth century. Each preacher considered is interpreted in the light of his environment, national as well as religious. A chronology of preachers is included in an appendix.

Petry, R. C. *Preaching in the Great Tradition: Neglected Chapters in the History of Preaching.* Philadelphia: The Westminister Press, 1950. A companion volume to the anthology of sermons the author selected and edited, *No Uncertain Sound,* gives the interpretive framework for the latter. Discusses and illustrates the tradition regarding the content of preaching in the years prior to the Reformation.

Webber, F. R. *A History of Preaching in Britain and America.* Milwaukee, Wis.: Northwestern Publishing House, 1952. This three-volume work covers a wealth of material, but the author's interpretation and criticism are often questionable inasmuch as they are based on a rigid view of evangelical preaching, a mechanical view of the atonement, a rhythmical view of history, and suspicion of biblical criticism.

Currier, A. H. *Nine Great Preachers.* New York: The Pilgrim Press, 1912. Emphasizes the personal qualities and spiritual character of such preachers as Chrysostom, Bernard, and Robertson. Its tone is more inspirational than critical. The power of preaching tends to be equated with the power of an inspired personality.

Blaikie, W. G. *The Preachers of Scotland from the Sixth to the Nineteenth Century.* Edinburgh: T. & T. Clark, 1888. Locates

218

the peculiar character and power of the Scottish pulpit in the remarkable combination of preaching and struggle throughout Scottish history. In Scotland, the message of redeeming grace was related to public struggles and movements, and this, the author contends, helps explain the thunderous tone of the Scottish pulpit. An illuminating study.

Smyth, C. *The Art of Preaching: A Practical Survey of Preaching in the Church of England, 747-1939*. London: SPCK, 1953. Consists primarily of tracing characteristic styles of preaching. Two lengthy and well-documented chapters on the style of the medieval sermon, its structure, language, and illustration, are particularly informative, as is the discussion of Tillotson's significance in the alteration of preaching style.

THE APOSTOLIC AND PATRISTIC PERIODS

Dodd, C. H. *The Apostolic Preaching and Its Development*. New York: Harper & Brothers, 1950. A basic work on the content of the apostolic proclamation. Contemporary discussions on the message of the early church still must reckon with Dodd's work.

Foster, J. *After the Apostles: Missionary Preaching of the First Three Centuries*. London: S. C. M. Press Ltd., 1951. Centers in the apologists of the second and third centuries, and quotes them generously on such subjects as the attack on polytheism, the use of the Bible, and the approach to the dominant intellectual currents of the time.

Kerr, H. T. *Preaching in the Early Church*. New York: Fleming H. Revell Co., 1942. Covers the period from the apostles to the fall of the Roman Empire. The preachers and the content of their sermons are interpreted properly in the context of church history. The repeated attempt to apply the wisdom of the past to the preacher of today is interesting at times, but somewhat superficial and distracting.

Weatherspoon, J. B. *Sent Forth to Preach: Studies in Apostolic Preaching*. New York: Harper & Brothers, 1954. Interrogates the New Testament for its answers to such questions as the nature, content, and purpose of preaching. The author's conclusions agree substantially with those of T. W. Manson and C. H. Dodd.

THE MEDIEVAL PERIOD

Neale, J. M. *Mediaeval Preachers and Mediaeval Preaching.* London: John and Charles Mozley, 1873. Following an informative and helpful introduction on the chief stylistic marks of medieval sermons, brief biographical sketches of the leading theologians and churchmen of the period together with quotations from their sermons are given.

Owst, G. R. *Literature and Pulpit in Medieval England: A Neglected Chapter in the History of English Letters and of the English People.* Second revised edition. Oxford: B. Blackwell, 1961. Traces out the often overlooked influence of the medieval pulpit on the history of letters. In a penetrating study, the author documents his claim that the pulpit was a creative center of literary satire, complaint, and secular drama. His discussion of the cultural significance of the *exempla* (sermon illustration) of the Middle Ages is exceptional.

_____. *Preaching in Medieval England: An Introduction to Sermon Manuscripts of the Period c. 1350-1450.* Cambridge: Cambridge University Press. 1926. A brilliant and thoroughly documented study of the preachers and sermons and other homiletical literature of the period seen in the context of social and religious life and thought. The treatment of mendicant preaching is unusually discerning and illuminating.

THE REFORMATION AND POST-REFORMATION PERIODS

Herr, A. F. *The Elizabethan Sermon: A Survey and A Bibliography.* Philadelphia: University of Pennsylvania, 1940. A published dissertation that surveys the sermons as a whole, and indicates the range of subject matter, the manner in which the sermons were preached, and the reception they received. The scope of the study, unfortunately, did not include theological analysis and criticism. Contains a comprehensive bibliography of the vast majority of printed Elizabethan sermons.

Kempe, J. E. *The Classic Preachers of the English Church.* New York: E. P. Dutton and Co., 1877. Discusses the celebrated preachers of the seventeenth century. These lectures are sermonic in tone and seek to expose the secret of greatness in each of the preachers. Lacks critical evaluation.

Kiessling, E. C. *The Early Sermons of Luther and Their Relation to the Pre-Reformation Sermon.* Grand Rapids, Mich.:

Zondervan Publishing House, 1935. Analyses Luther's sermons through 1522, and shows the influence of scholasticism, mysticism, and Luther's own theological revolution on the structure and content of his sermons. This scholarly study focusses the central message of the Reformation proclamation by tracing its emergence in Luther's sermons and by contrasting it with pre-Reformation influences and sermons.

Levy, B. M. *Preaching in the First Half Century of New England History.* Hartford, Conn.: The American Society of Church History, 1945. This published dissertation is by far the best available study of early American Puritan preaching. The doctrine, style, and form of sermons are thoroughly investigated, and both the condition of the churches and the spirit of the times are sympathetically described. Corrects some common misconceptions of Puritan preaching.

Mitchell, W. F. *English Pulpit Oratory from Andrews to Tillotson: A Study of Its Literary Aspects.* London: SPCK, 1932. A comprehensive study of the sermons of seventeenth-century preachers from the standpoint of homiletical theory, homiletical practice, and criticism of sermons. Traces the evolution of English prose style through what the author calls "witty" preaching (Andrewes) and "metaphysical" preaching (Donne), with criticism of both. Theological bias is shown to be a major factor in determining style. Volume contains an excellent bibliography on preaching manuals, sermon manuscripts, and sermon criticisms of the period.

Richardson, C. F. *English Preachers and Preaching, 1640-1670.* New York: The Macmillan Co., 1928. During this period of intense religious controversy, thought, and behavior, the author shows the preachers to be neither so dull nor so doctrinaire as tradition has branded them. The human, everyday side of the preachers is stressed. Contains a helpful bibliography.

THE MODERN PERIOD

Brastow, L. O. *Representative Modern Preachers.* New York: The Macmillan Co., 1904. Contains an excellent selection of nineteenth-century preachers, including Schleiermacher, Robertson, and Newman. Supplies biographical information and discusses each preacher's basic theological position, central sermonic themes, and characteristic style.

Davies, H. *Varieties of English Preaching, 1900-1960.* Englewood Cliffs, N. J.: Prentice-Hall, Inc., 1963. Analyses the religious thought and preaching style of fourteen eminent preachers who are grouped under eight different types of preaching. Faithfully mirrors the revolutions in theological persuasion and preaching styles of this period, and offers perceptive criticisms of each man's preaching.

Hoyt, A. S. *The Pulpit and American Life.* New York: The Macmillan Co., 1921. Emphasizes the social and political significance of the pulpit in American life. Selects preachers who have been most prophetic and directive of spiritual and social advance, and discusses them in the light of their message and personality. Somewhat dated theologically.

Jones, E. D. *The Royalty of the Pulpit.* New York: Harper & Brothers, 1951. Surveys the Lyman Beecher Lectures on preaching, and gives a vivid and moving account of each lecturer. Characteristics of his preaching and the major thrust of his lectures also are discussed. This series of lectures is a rich quarry which will reward the student who works it.

McGraw, J. *Great Evangelical Preachers of Yesterday.* Nashville: Abingdon Press, 1961. Although this volume begins with Wycliffe, it contains a discussion of many nineteenth-century evangelists and their preaching. The author's view of evangelism is somewhat naive and mechanical, but many of his interpretations are instructive. Contains a bibliography on the preachers discussed.

Pipes, W. H. *Say Amen, Brother.* New York: The William-Frederick Press, 1951. A study of old-time Negro preaching, based on tape recordings of sermons from churches in Macon County, Georgia. The author gives an interpretation of the influences which shaped it and stamped it with its unique character. He is also preaching a contemporary sermon through this study!

Thompson, E. T. *Changing Emphases in American Preaching.* Philadelphia: The Westminister Press, 1943. These lectures interpret the theological and ecclesiastical significance of Bushnell, Beecher, Moody, Gladden, and Rauschenbusch on the American pulpit. A careful and judicious statement of the central beliefs of each man is given, and his influence on preaching is elaborated.

COLLECTIONS OF SERMONS

None of the many volumes of sermons by individual preachers has been included in this list. There are simply too many. The five volumes which are mentioned contain good selections, cover the period, and are fairly accessible.

Blackwood, Andrew W. *The Protestant Pulpit*. Nashville: Abingdon-Cokesbury Press, 1947. An anthology of sermons since the Reformation. A good, representative selection.

Fish, H. C. *History and Repository of Pulpit Eloquence*. New York: Dodd, Mead & Co., 1877. The largest and best selection in a single book. Includes historical surveys of preaching in different countries, biographical sketches of the preachers, and critical notes on the sermons.

Kleiser, G. *World's Great Sermons*. New York: Funk and Wagnalls Co., 1908. Ten short volumes introduced by L. O. Brastow. Each sermon is prefaced by a short biographical sketch of the preacher.

Macartney, C. E. *Great Sermons of the World*. Boston, Mass.: The Stratford Co., 1926. Great sermons are sermons of great men, and great men are men greatly known!—so reasons the editor.

Petry, R. C. *No Uncertain Sound: Sermons That Shaped the Pulpit Tradition*. Philadelphia: The Westminister Press, 1948. An excellent introduction discusses that tradition, and the illustrative sermons are selected from a period extending from the second century to the Reformation.

223

INDEX OF NAMES

225

THE PREACHER'S PAPERBACK LIBRARY

Volumes already published:

1. *The Servant of the Word* by H. H. Farmer. 1964.

2. *The Care of the Earth and Other University Sermons* by Joseph Sittler. 1964.

3. *The Preaching of F. W. Robertson* edited by Gilbert E. Doan, Jr. 1964.

4. *A Brief History of Preaching* by Yngve Brilioth (translated by Karl E. Mattson). 1965.

Further volumes are in preparation.

Type, 10 on 12 Garamond
Display, Garamond
Paper, Standard Antique GM